What Others Are Saying About This Book

▼

"I really enjoyed it. I read it in Niagara Falls and then with a plane cancellation coming home there was a mix up and I was the only Dallas passenger who didn't get moved to another plane so I sat 12 hours in an airport. After reading your book I negotiated a free upgrade so I was treated like a queen coming back."

— Patti Logan, EA, NTPI Instructor and NTPI 2002 Dean

"I just finished reading your book for the second time and found it informative with a refreshing humorous approach. Yesterday I would have negotiated from a weak spot, but using some of your tactics I turned around and attacked the IRS like they were on the defensive. I ended up getting everything I wanted . . . plus a little extra. Thanks again for the enjoyment and lessons I learned."

— David M. Levine, EA^{MGF}, Chair,
NTPI Graduate Fellows Association

"I'm speechless."

— Robert A. Payne, Former President
Toastmasters International, Incline Village, NV

"Bobby Covic's book, *Everything's Negotiable!* entertains while teaching negotiating skills that can help anyone pay less for everyday goods and services."

— E. Ann Shroll, EA^{F}, President, NAEA, 2001-2002

"If anyone knows . . . ins and outs it's Bobby Covic. An important resource for any executive or service worker."

— Delores Marconi, Publisher of *Deal Magazine*

" . . . informative and fun to read!"

— Lynda R. Paulson, Author of *The Executive Persuader, How to be a Powerful Speaker*

" . . . enjoy . . . tales of deal making . . . in everyday circumstances . . . easy reading . . . pick up some pointers that will help you save money . . ."

— Carol Petit, EA, Book Reviewer, *EA Journal*

"WOW! Bobby really nails it with his funny stories. I'm already getting more of what I want by using these techniques! This one's a winner!"

— Chloe A. Parham, MFCC

"I don't think you can do any better than Bobby Covic. Quite simply, he's the best!"

— Morgan D. King, Attorney and Author, *Discharging Taxes in Bankruptcy: Law and Practice*

"...useful words of wisdom, practical tips and secrets for winning communications . . . a great read on a warm summer afternoon . . . just plain fun . . ."

— R. Michael "Mickey" Reedy, EA^{MFG}, NTPI Instructor, Graduate Fellows Officer

EVERYTHING'S NEGOTIABLE!

How to Bargain Better
To Get What You Want

Bobby Covic, EA

Third Edition

Pendulum Publishing • Incline Village, Nevada

Everything's Negotiable!
How to Bargain Better To Get What You Want
by Bobby Covic, EA

Published by:
Pendulum Publishing
Post Office Box 6206
Incline Village, Nevada 89450, U.S.A.
775-831-7694 • 888-687-8197
bobbycovic@aol.com • www.bobbycovic.com

Editor: Helene Yates

Caricature: Mark Seagraves, MarkDSea@aol.com; www.caricaturenow.com

Cover Art Production: Robb Pawlak, Pawlak Designs

Back Cover Photo: John Thomas, Thomas Photography, Incline Village, Nevada

Everything's Negotiable! is meant to be fun and educational only. The author is not rendering legal, accounting or other professional advice or services herein. You are encouraged to enhance your bargaining capabilities further by checking out the list of relevant resources in the back.

The author and publishing company shall have neither liability nor responsibility to any person or entity with respect to any loss or damage caused, or alleged to be caused directly or indirectly, by the information contained in this book. If you do not wish to be bound by the above, you may return this book to the publisher for a full refund.

Printed in the United States of America

Covic, Bobby.
Everything's negotiable! : how to bargain better to get what you want / Bobby Covic. -- 3rd ed.
p. cm.
Includes bibliographical references.
LCCN 2003103722
ISBN 0-9710855-1-X

1. Negotiation. 2. Success. I. Title.

BF637.N4C68 2003 158.1
QBI33-1254

Dedication

This book is dedicated to my loving family.

First and foremost, I'd like to thank my beautiful, loyal and encouraging wife, Marti. Without her unfailing emotional support I would have lacked the confidence to "put pen to paper" in the first place.

Thanks to my dear mom, Shirley, for teaching me that it doesn't hurt to ask. Thanks to my infinitely patient Dad, Lt. Col. Donald M. Covic, for inadvertently teaching me how to circumvent higher authority. He was truly an officer and a gentleman.

Thanks to my two sweet sisters, Susan and Debbie, for humoring me and putting up with my tomfoolery for the last half-century or so.

Acknowledgments

Many good folks contributed to the creation of this book. Unfortunately, space and memory limit my ability to express my appreciation to everyone who helped turn a dream into a reality.

Thanks to my most cherished pal and office manager since 1989, Carol Johnson. Without her stability, unwavering dedication and good ol' matter-of-fact Midwestern temperament, the daily trials of self-employment would probably have gotten the best of me by now.

I'd like to extend a very special thanks to my editor extraordinaire, the consummate Helene Yates. I asked and she did it. And, she did it with style, panache and class. "H.Y." served as editor, hand-holder, webmaster, computer tamer, graphic artist, marketing maven, etc. With Helene, the impossible only took a little longer.

Thanks to Bill Judd for keeping my computers hummin' since 1984. To my good buddies, Bob Payne and Mark Pilarski, thanks for keeping ol' Bobby C. going through the ups and downs.

Thanks to all the real-life characters in all the stories in *Everything's Negotiable!* There wouldn't have been any stories without you. Drew, Rick, Katrina, Marti, et. al. Thanks to (yes, I really mean this!) even the IRS for giving me the daily challenge of "Battling the Beast".

And, last but (by far) not least, thanks to my dearly departed office cat, Mel. Your spirit will always be with me. You taught me to keep "meowing" until I get what I want. God bless you, Mel - you were truly one in a billion.

Authorities and sources are listed at the end of this book.

"Everything's negotiable!"

— Bobby Covic, EA

Table of Contents

Table of Contents continued. . .

Foreword

Bobby Covic's *Everything's Negotiable!* has to be one of the most informative and enjoyable books I have read on the subject of negotiation. *Everything's Negotiable!* provides a friendly bridge between the intimidating world of professional negotiation and the familiar world of Saturday afternoon garage sale bargaining.

Bobby is now in his third successful decade representing clients with nightmarish IRS problems. His "David v. Goliath" experiences assure you'll profit from the vital advice conveyed in his stories. He also hits upon an idea that is largely missing in civilized society — being friendly and polite.

This has to be one of the best books I've read in a long time, both professionally and personally. You'll love the easy way Bobby helps you understand the elegance of his results-oriented tricks of the trade. If you've always wanted to be a winner in the transactions of everyday life, you've got the right book in your hands.

Enjoy!

— *William J. Downey, President*
International Association of Professional Negotiators

INTRODUCTION

It is said that truth is *stranger* than fiction. This collection of true stories from Bobby Covic proves that truth can also be far more *entertaining* than fiction.

From these real-people experiences, these all-true stories, anyone and everyone can glean valuable skills. These skills give you practical advantages and help increase opportunities for you to emerge triumphant in everyday challenges.

In realms as varied as shopping, traveling and customer service, Bobby Covic provides you with simple, user-friendly approaches and tactics that lead you to success.

As I edited this book, I found myself using these time-honored techniques and sharing them with others. Bobby uses his delightful stories to impart valuable knowledge in neat little packages; ready to help you be the master of your own life (and wallet!).

This book does what it claims to do. It empowers both the less-experienced and the brightest folks to feel more confident, to know that they really did their best to get what they want for less. Another big bonus is — it's fun to read!

Editing this book has been a sincere pleasure. I might not otherwise have learned these new and useful skills, and I had a great time doing it!

—Helene Yates, Editor

Preface

This book is designed to share entertaining success stories with you and to reveal simple techniques to make your life more rewarding.

What is most important to you? It might be love, money or fame. It might be power or serenity. It might even be just preventing that car salesman from getting the best of you. Well, whatever it is — you've come to the right place.

This little book will help you get what you want. The best way to use it is simply to read and enjoy it. The techniques in the true stories I'm sharing with you here will come to your aid when you need them. They will come naturally and easily if you just read and enjoy.

Although you can learn how to get more of what you want by reading these true stories, there is no magic wand here, no absolute guarantees.

Read and enjoy. That's all you have to do. What you can get out of this book will amaze you. The sky's the limit. Happy Better Bargaining!

— Bobby Covic, EA, Incline Village, Nevada

I NEGOTIATE THEREFORE I AM
BY
R.R. "BOBBY" COVIC
©Mark Scognone 1997

1

What's in It for Me?

If you're like most of us worker ants, you're incredibly busy. In this information-intensive age, you probably don't have the time or patience to digest one more "bit" of new information without first knowing what's in it for you.

That said, I'm sure if you'll invest just a few moments of your precious time with me, you'll get a BIG payoff. You'll benefit with better tomorrows, more control over your life and more money. If that sounds good to you, keep reading.

My name is R.R. "Bobby" Covic, EA, but you can call me Bobby. I'm a professional negotiator. My goal is to empower you to even up the odds in your life. How can you benefit? Just answer these three questions.

- ☛ Do you ever feel like you are getting the short end of life's stick?
- ☛ Do you ever feel like a David in Goliath's world?
- ☛ Would you like to change the "balance of power" between you and them?

If you answered yes to any of those questions, you're in for a treat. You can learn to negotiate your way through life like a pro. You probably already have a wealth of hidden negotiating talents and abilities that are just in need of a little polish.

How can I help you? What are my credentials? And — what's that "EA" behind my name?

Help

I will give you simple, yet powerful, negotiation techniques. You can start using these immediately to turn the tide of events in your life.

Credentials

I'm a '69 U.C. "Bezerkeley" (Berkeley) grad (Psychology). Former careers: professional musician, vocational rehabilitation counselor, real estate salesperson/broker/investor/landlord and casino craps dealer.

EA (Enrolled Agent)

I am an EA specializing in taxpayer advocacy. EA's are federally licensed tax professionals admitted to represent clients before the IRS in the same manner as CPA's or attorneys.

Memberships

International Association of Professional Negotiators (Charter Member), National Association of Enrolled Agents and National Speakers Association.

So, let's get started. It's a fact . . . everything's negotiable. "Oh, sure," you might say, "but what about death and taxes?" Well, I have to admit, I'm still working on the former but taxes . . . ah, that's another story. Here's a recent "taxes are negotiable" anecdote.

AB owed IRS for two years. She retained me to represent her. The total due with interest and penalties was around $30,000 ($30K) when we struck the deal. Deal? Yes, deal! IRS has a program called Offer in Compromise. The law (IRC § 7122) allows the Feds to "compromise" a delinquent tax debt. You must show that either:

- ✔ the tax was assessed in error,
- ✔ you don't have the ability to pay, or
- ✔ it would create an economic hardship for you to pay.

Enough of the facts and rules. Guess what IRS settled for? Not $20K; not even $10K. Hold on to your hats now, friends . . . IRS settled for $100. That's right! 100 measly greenbacks. Imagine. $30K went away for the price of a fancy pair of tennis shoes . . . and you always heard that taxes aren't negotiable!

LESSON 1

Don't believe everything you hear.

LESSON 2

Don't ever be afraid to involve a professional.

If you owe the Feds and want to make an offer, call IRS at 1-800-829-1040 to see if you might qualify.

Three Sayings to Forget:

1. Assume: makes an "ass" out of "u" and "me"
2. Never assume anything.
3. Always assume the worst.

2

The Assumptive Approach

It was a sizzling, summer afternoon in muggy central California. Richard was going into 9th grade; I was ready for 8th. We needed immediate relief from this temperature torture. A matinee at the air-conditioned, dark Castle Air Force Base theatre would work!

It was always "bargain city" . . . probably a quarter, max, to see a double-feature. Creative problem-solvers that we were, we hitched a ride and dragged our young behinds up to the theatre. Always playing the fool, I admonished ol' Rick to stop as he dug deep into his jeans pocket for 25¢. "I'll betcha I can get us in here free!" I boasted. Always up to a "Merry Prankster" caper, Rick readied himself for the strategy.

It was almost show time and we weren't the only two Einsteins who had solved the equation of beating the heat by catching a flick. A bunch of sweaty fellow cinema fans stood in one slow-motion line to purchase tickets and then stood in yet another to give an usher their heat-relief-passes.

Standing in line looked like a drag. Saving a quarter sounded like a winner. Then, the idea hit me like a sun blast on an ice cube. "Follow me, Rick. Walk fast. Keep your head down. Don't say ANYTHING. Once we're inside, keep walkin'."

We fell into the second line. The usher was busily ripping tickets, keeping half, and sending paying customers through the turnstile. A quarter poorer each, inside they went with ticket stub passports to Frigid Air Nirvana — cinematic heaven.

I could feel my heart beating faster. I know my face was red as a beet in the heat. Time had come — our turn. I assumed the posture of authority. My gait quickened. My pal shadowed my moves. I avoided eye contact with the usher and, in a rush of ridiculous bravado, I turned my hand palm-up as if to show some sort of ID. As confidently as I could, I asserted "PRESS", made sure my buddy was close on my tail, and kept movin'.

An 8th grader and a 9th grader. I'm sure he really thought we were media men. Right!

Then, my heart started beating even faster; we were in!!! Incredible. We did it. My pal blushed and then beamed. But, then "what-ifs" started creeping in; glee immediately subsided. I could just hear siren screams from the blue trucks of the base police. I could imagine the cold, steel handcuffs as they dragged us off, back into the blazing oven outside and into the interrogation room. My Dad was not going to be happy.

"Keep your head down and keep walking," I said to myself. Past the snack bar; into the dark. Rick mirrored my moves. WE WERE HOME FREE!

We grabbed a couple of seats, cooled our heels and chilled out in the safety of the darkness. Only moments passed until we were slapping our knees in muted laughter. We couldn't believe it; it worked! We pulled it off! We still laugh about that silliness.

LESSON

Foolishness of this story aside, try using the assumptive approach. Assume a posture of authority. Posture power! Assume that your approach is going to fly. Visualize yourself on the other side of the turnstile of your current negotiation. Believe that you belong where you're trying to go.

Most importantly, keep your head down and keep walking. Maybe you'll draw lucky like we did. Sometimes, if you try something ridiculous and outrageous enough, the ushers of life will be so amused, astounded and awe-stricken with mirth that they'll let you go through without even paying the quarter.

> *"No one should drive a hard bargain with an artist."*
>
> — Ludwig von Beethoven

3

Courtly Language of Negotiation

"Do you think there might be any chance?"
— Drew Sallee

He sang and played sax. I was fat and played drums. We had a great band named "Drew Sallee and the Dead" (several years BEFORE the Grateful Dead). He was kind of a street kid. I lived on an Air Force base; my father was Lt. Colonel D.M. Covic, U.S.A.F., a "well-respected man." Drew and I were only 17. He knew how to negotiate; I didn't.

We needed a place to rehearse. We were loud, and our entourage wasn't a pretty sight. Drew had orange hair and an eye patch. He looked like a Crazy Count Dracula in his purple velvet-lined, black cape and knee-high patent leather boots. We traveled in two long, black hearses, looking like funeral-procession-meets-Alice-Cooper, arriving on the scene about 10 years early. The Wooten Brothers, two 300-pound truck drivers, doubled as our security and equipment schleppers. Death wagon cargo included instruments and stage props: a "real-life" coffin, tombstones, a human skull, etc.

Obviously, our parents weren't fighting over who would host rehearsals. Mine lived in the "Officers' Quarters" section. Our neighbors were Brigadier Generals and the like. My house was an unlikely candidate for "The Morbid Sounds of Drew Sallee and the Dead" rehearsals.

Nevertheless, Drew approached me one dark night after a graveyard band meeting. "Hey, Big Bob . . ." (Now I want you to pay particular attention to these words.) "I was wonderin', do you think there might be any chance that your folks might consider letting us rehearse at your house?"

Whoa — this was my first introduction to (what I'd later realize was) the smooth, gracious and courtly language of negotiation. Drew was an entry-level, silver-tongued devil; subtle and slick in his own street-smart kind of way. Let's examine Drew's approach.

Hey, Big Bob

He summoned my attention. The most beautiful sound in the world to a person is the sound of his or her own name. The nickname adds an extra element of affection.

I was wonderin'

This is a very disarming and non-threatening way to begin. It expresses curiosity. It sounds like a very innocent query is coming up. In reality, it is the set-up for a "trial balloon" — your reaction is going to be tested.

Do you think there might be any chance

This seeks an opinion. Everyone is flattered to be consulted for an opinion. This does not actually ask for anything. Drew only solicited my opinion about whether, in my obviously valued opinion, a possibility existed. A *possibility* almost always exists that just about anything could happen at just about any time.

That your folks might consider

He didn't ask if my folks would actually let us rehearse at their house, only whether (I thought) they *might consider* it. Well, who could dispute that someone might consider something? Certainly there existed some possibility that my folks *might* consider it.

Letting us rehearse at your house?

Taking into account Drew's masterful set-up, statistics and probability, there isn't another potentially correct answer to his well-structured question besides YES.

Long story short: With great fear and trepidation, I asked my most-esteemed parents and, surprisingly, they agreed. There was only one proviso — Drew would never be allowed to be alone in any room in the house with my beautiful 15-year-old sister.

LESSON

The language of negotiation is courtly, subtle and smooth. It isn't blunt or even necessarily direct. Utilize Drew's winning set-up or a version of your own. Say your "opponent's" name. Express your curiosity. Use a trial balloon. Query your opponent's opinion. Inquire about possibilities. Be prepared to hear the word *YES!*

"Everything absolute belongs in pathology."

— Friedrich Nietzsche

4

If it Ain't Broke - Don't Buy It

"Everything's broken." — Bob Dylan

Here's a technique I call "The Defect". It works like this:

FIRST

Find something you would like to buy in a store.

THEN

Inspect it like a jeweler looking for a flaw in a fine diamond. Remember, nothing's perfect; just about everything has a noticeable defect.

NEXT

Approach the shopkeeper to obtain a discount that will reflect the diminished value.

You'll get a kick out of this true story that demonstrates the "If It Ain't Broke — Don't Buy It" proviso.

After a speaking engagement near Denver, I was hangin' out with my buds, Tom and Danny. Tom wanted to find a nice gift for his bedridden wife. We were in "Outlet City" and ended up at a store that sells china, fine crystal and related unnecessary knick-knacks. My buddies are always kidding me about my obsession with negotiation. Anyway, Tom finally found a beautiful crystal vase that was marked down from $89.99 to $49.99. He handed it to me with a friendly challenge: "Okay, Bobby, let's see you do your stuff."

Gee, I actually thought $49.99 was a pretty good deal already. Golly, it had been marked down by 45%. I am aware of a business principle out there somewhere postulating that a store must make a profit to stay in business. I didn't see a "Going Out of Business" sign in the window. So, it was crystal clear; I definitely had my work cut out for me.

Ah, but you know what's coming next! That's right — the obligatory inspection for "The Defect". Well, lo and behold, I found it. There it was, almost invisible to the naked eye, but it was there. Tom could hardly see it; no way would his wife ever notice it. What might have looked like a tiny imperfection in the glass to most folks looked like golden opportunity to me.

The performance began. With a somewhat dejected expression on my face, I took the vase to the counter. I was interested in buying it but I was sorrowful that it was defective. To make matters worse, it was the last one on display. I made eye contact with the nice young woman behind the counter, smiled, offered my hand and introduced myself. I gave her my business card, pointed out "The Defect" and asked if she had the authority to extend a discount to offset the diminished value.

She didn't have authority, but was pleased to introduce Rick, the manager, who did. She apprised him of the situation.

"Rick, I'd really like to buy this but I'm uncomfortable with the defect. I don't want to insult you, but is there any way you would consider taking $25?" He smiled and retorted: "Let me look it up on our inventory list and I will help you if I can." His research apparently told him that he had room to maneuver. "How does $19.99 sound?" Well, need I say more? A $90 piece for $21.49 including tax — my math says that's a discount of about 88%.

I jokingly said, "If you have another one of those in the back somewhere Rick, I'd be happy to take it off your hands for the same price." To my surprise, he sent the nice sales woman to the back, and she returned with an identical vase (with no defect) and now I had a beautiful gift for my wife. Double bonus!

LESSON

If It Ain't Broke — Don't Buy It. As Bob Dylan said, "Everything's broken." Just look for the defect. Smile, make eye contact, personalize yourself with an introduction and don't forget your Visa.

"If only I had known I should have become a watchmaker."

— Albert Einstein

5

Reduction to the Ridiculous

"For just pennies a day . . ."

She did it — without even knowing it! Reduction to the Ridiculous — Just like a pro. Ah, but let me start at the beginning.

My lovely assistant Marlene needed help negotiating a personal injury claim with an insurance company. In part, she argued that, due to her injury, her husband lost 80 hours of work. He had to drive her to the doctor, etc. Well, at hubby's hourly pay of $25, she was asking for an additional $2,000 (80 X $25). I thought: no way, no how.

She began explaining. It was as though she had a specific genetic predisposition to negotiation genius. "Bobby, look," she started, "over a four-month period, 80 hours is only 20 hours a month. Only five-hours a week. That's only one-hour a day. Twenty-five lousy bucks a day, that's nothing."

Reduction to the Ridiculous — A Negotiation Classic

Marlene did it naturally. She backed the numbers down. She shifted my focus from $2,000 to the low, low cost of $25. She reduced the BIG number to a ridiculously small number.

I could see it. She gave me the ammo I needed to make it sound reasonable to the claims adjuster. Psychologically, it made it easy for him to say yes. After all, what's $25 a day? It worked like a charm!

You hear this all the time. TV infomercials are famous for Reduction to the Ridiculous. It's easy to get sucked in. You start to rationalize. "Gee, $89.99 payable over three months. That's only $29.99 a month, less than a dollar a day. I can't even buy a cup of coffee at 7-Eleven for that. Where's the phone? Hand me that VISA. I'm gonna own that whiz-bang techno-gizmo." It's embarrassing. We've all fallen for this one.

The Reverse Reduction to the Ridiculous — The Classic Turned Inside Out

Car salespersons and real estate folks use Reduction to the Ridiculous shamelessly. See how you can turn it around.

John and Mary Newhouse are house hunting. Their budget is really tight. The absolute most they can possibly afford for a monthly payment is $850. And that's with everything: principal, interest, taxes, insurance, etc.

Their friend, Andrea Agent, finds them "the perfect house". One problem. The monthly hit will be $875. "We just can't do it," pleads John. "Sure you can," reasons Andrea, "The difference is only $25 a month. That's nothing. $6.25 a week: Eighty-three cents a day. Come on, John? Surely you wouldn't let eighty-three cents a day come between your dear wife and the house of her dreams?"

Now John uses the Reverse Reduction to the Ridiculous. He turns the old classic inside out on Andrea. First, he calls her on it, and lets her know he knows what she's doing.

"Andrea, please, don't use Reduction to the Ridiculous on me. You know, that eighty-three cents a day really adds up over the life of a 30-year loan. Let's see, eighty-three cents a day — (here comes the reverse) that's $25 a month; that's $300 a year; that's

$9,000 over the life of the loan! If we were to invest eighty-three cents a day at a rate of even 6% interest compounding annually over 30 years, do you realize how much we'd have?" Andrea gags. She knows he knows the game. He lays the figure on her. $23,717.46! Point well taken, Andrea blushes and starts looking for a more affordable house.

LESSON

Figures lie and liars figure. Don't let 'em massage the numbers and play games with you. You're too smart for that! Call 'em on it and hit 'em with the reverse.

> *"Another victory like that and we're done for."*
>
> — Pyrrhus, Plutarch's Lives

6

The Flinch: "He Wanted 400% More"

My former secretary, KJ, was young and shy when she came to work for me. Her shyness didn't last long though. I taught her the negotiation "tricks of the trade" from day one.

KJ was only 13 when I started training her in the fine art of getting what you want. Here's an example of one of the deals she made. Keep in mind, this is the kind of deal you can make too — EVERY DAY!!!

KJ's assignment was to get the Velcro repaired on one of my sandals. As she left for the local shoe repair shop, my parting words to her were: " . . . don't let 'em charge you too much."

The shop owner repaired it while she waited. He then plopped the revitalized Teva down on the counter in front of her. "$12," he announced. The power now shifted. KJ had learned her negotiation lessons well. She proceeded to overwhelm the unsuspecting owner with three simple, yet powerful techniques.

- **THE FLINCH.**

  She radically changed her posture. She FLINCHED. Her body-language said: "I'm stunned." She became rigid as if having just been hit with a sucker punch.

  She looked astonished, astounded and confused. She conveyed the overall demeanor of disbelief. The flinch creates doubt in the mind of the seller.

- **"THAT'S TOO MUCH!"**

  She parroted the precise power phrase I taught her. She asserted confidently: "THAT'S TOO MUCH." And then, she concluded her performance with one of the most effective techniques known (especially to womankind). She shut up. Men tend to have a little trouble with this one. We guys tend to want to "keep selling after the sale."

- **THE SILENT TREATMENT.**

  KJ simply shut up. She exercised discipline. Mum was the magic word. The silence was deafening. The pressure mounted. The owner caved in.

Now listen to the beautiful sound of his voluntary response, and the ensuing interactions.

Owner: "Okay, $3."

KJ: "Great. Thank-you very much."

Me: "You got it done for $3? Fantastic, KJ. Incredible job!"

This is a classic win-win situation; the shopkeeper got a satisfied customer, the best advertising money can buy, and KJ got a great deal.

Now, just imagine if your every economic encounter could save you money like that. The shopkeeper originally asked for 400% more than he was actually willing to settle for ($12 divided by $3 = 4 times). All KJ did was (1) flinch, (2) assert, and (3) shut up. So easy even a child could do it. Matter of fact, children are just naturally good at these three techniques. Give this approach a try. I personally feel it will keep your money in your pocket WHERE IT BELONGS.

Now, let's conclude by talking about scale. In the example above, even though the percentage of savings (400%) was large, we're really only talking about nine actual dollars saved. So what's the big deal? Well, it is all really a matter of scale. If you perfect the techniques in the example, they will work equally well in larger dollar situations.

KEY

Practice on the small stuff. Then, when it comes time to negotiate for a big-ticket item, your skills will already be finely honed. Your expertise will be second nature to you. You'll surprise yourself at the success you will realize using the flinch!

LESSON

Every day is filled with opportunities to become a better bargainer by using the principles you learn in this book. Start small. Flinch, assert, shut-up and enjoy the benefits on a larger and larger scale as you perfect your skills.

> *"Good judgment comes from experience,*
> *which comes from bad judgment."*
>
> — Rudy McDaniel, Entrepreneur

7

"You're Pushin' Too Hard"

— Sky Saxon, The Seeds

Sometimes you just gotta know when to back off! Here's an embarrassing example. One Thanksgiving I flew from Reno to Las Vegas to spend the holiday with my wife's family. My dear wife Marti arrived earlier but was considerate enough to reserve a rental car for me. As a matter of fact, well trained by the master, she had negotiated a darn good rate on it!

I took the airport courtesy van to Hertz. It was hot, crowded and I was anxious to get my car and drive to my in-laws' house to relax. There were a gazillion people in town and a million of them were standing in line in front of me. Nonetheless, finally, it was my turn. Up to the counter I strolled.

Hallelujah! My name came right up on the reservation computer. The agent quoted me the exact rate I was expecting. All was going perfectly. But wait! Everything's negotiable, right? Right! So, you got it, I went into action. Watch this now — a consummate professional at work.

"How much better can you do for me on that rate?" I asked the unwary female. She stonewalled me.

"That's the rate the car was reserved at and that's the best rate I can give you," she responded impatiently. No problem, I thought. "Who has the authority to extend me the courtesy of a better rate?" I asked assertively. She shot back angrily: "Only the owner." Oh, I know this one — the old "resort to higher authority" gambit. Not to worry.

"Great! I'll speak to the owner." She was getting totally steamed by now. The people in back of me were getting bugged. She snapped back with intensity: "Sir, the owner is not here. Do you want the car or not?" I couldn't believe what I was hearing. Whatever happened to customer service in this country anyway?

I wasn't about to be brushed off that easily. I let her know I didn't like her attitude. I demanded that she get the owner on the phone immediately. The heat was getting to me; I was feeling stressed. She refused to call the manager. I guess I must have raised my voice a little for effect. Undaunted, I asked for her name and employee number, telling her I was going to write a complaint letter.

I knew that would get her attention; she'd surely succumb to the pressure, call the owner and get me a respectable discount. I'd be happily on my way in short order. Just like clockwork, she left the counter and picked up the phone. I felt triumphant! She'd caved in and I'd won!

But nooooo, negotiation master. She was calling the cops. Yeah, the cops! I could actually hear her ask them to send a unit immediately to arrest an irate customer who was disturbing the peace.

Well, no need for that kind of action. I apologized sheepishly and plopped the ol' Visa down on the counter. I reasoned that no discount could be worth spending Turkey Day in the slammer over. But then (can you believe this?) she refused to take my credit card. Now, she wouldn't even rent me the car. I was mortified.

She was serious. I had two choices. (1) Wait around to be arrested, or (2) Take the courtesy van back to the airport. Guess what I did? That's right. Back to square one. Thanksgiving. Swarms of people in Las Vegas. 110° in the shade. Tail between my legs, off I went looking for 35¢ to call Marti and explain why I'd be a little late.

Sometimes you just gotta know when to back off!

"No matter what we personally want,
we have to pay the price with our time."

— Anonymous

8

The Artificial Time Crisis

"We want the world and we want it now."
— Jim Morrison

"We want the world and we want it now," Morrison screamed in the Doors' classic, "When the Music's Over". The anthem of baby boomers, the American way. As wanna-be negotiators, it's often our downfall. We tend to want everything, right now.

Faster computers and the Internet produce immediate information. Pre-approved credit cards allow us easy access. Waiting does not compute. Instant gratification is the internal battle cry. Uncertainty threatens to create anxiety; anxiety translates to discomfort, and, in the good 'ol U.S. of A., discomfort is not tolerable. We'd rather pay more now and numb that pain than exercise the patience that good negotiation requires.

Advertising exploits this to the hilt; it still succeeds with the age-old "AIDA" formula shown on the following page.

We're manipulated gracefully (almost subliminally) through this. Generally, by the time we enter into a negotiation for a purchase, we desperately need to recover from the advertiser's spell of "AIDA" with the help of a good credit counselor!

AIDA FORMULA

A = Attention

Grab their attention.

I = Interest

Spark their interest.

D = Desire

Ignite their passion; create desire for the product.

A = Action

Get them to act — NOW.

Problem

At this point, we're like lambs led to slaughter. All a savvy salesperson needs to do now to get our hard-earned dollars is, simply, get us to act.

Here's the hook. Salespersons are Master Button Pushers. They know which of our psychological and emotional buttons make us act.

We're all vulnerable on some level. All of us have suffered loss. Loss hurts. We're all motivated to avoid pain — at almost any cost. Enter the slick sales technique of "the artificial time crisis" and its ugly sister, "the take-away".

I fell victim to this one-two punch. My car mechanic advised me to get a new car *immediately*. "You're going to blow a rod" sounded pretty bad to me. It made me hurry (first mistake). And then came "AIDA".

AIDA IN ACTION

Attention:

The TV ad got my attention.

Interest:

Just the macho machine I'd always wanted — sleek, black, new and fast.

Desire:

The guy on the phone ignited my desire — it was "on sale".

Action:

He catapulted me into action.

Punch One

The artificial time crisis. "You'd better get down here quickly. It's the only one we have."

Punch Two

The take-away. "I don't want you to miss out. A woman called just before you and she's coming down later to check it out."

Salespersons use this deadly duo of punches on the unsuspecting to evoke immediate action. We "react" to the ploy like marionettes on strings. We act, and our action produces the sale. The consummation of the sale alleviates us of the anxiety and uncertainty of waiting. The mystery is then over, and as my old friend and former real estate broker Rudy McDaniel used to say, "When a man with money meets a man with experience, the man with the money gets the experience and the man with the experience gets the money."

In this case, I was the man with the money meeting the man with the experience. I got the car; he got the money. He got me to act by pushing the right buttons and using two sales classics, "the artificial time crisis" and "the take-away".

LESSONS

Take your time; don't fall for these old Carney tricks. There's always another sleek, black, new and fast something on sale (and probably cheaper) somewhere. And . . . sometimes the woman who was supposed to come down after work doesn't ever show.

9

When Not to Negotiate

"Honey, please don't get too tricky . . ."

Streams on both sides, surrounded by National Forest, within walking distance of Lake Tahoe, a dream cottage in paradise. My dear wife, Marti, loved everything about it. It was right out of a fairy tale.

Marti and I are a great real estate team: she picks out the property and I figure out how we're going to pay for it.

All kidding aside, Marti does her homework. She had been watching for something like this for a long time. She saw the ad the first day it hit the paper. Remembering the three keys to successful real estate investment — location, location, location — Marti knew the value was there, even at list price.

She gave me the details. The owner had just listed it. It was going to move fast. Not wanting to see Marti's sweet heart broken, I shot into action. Our Realtor, Shahri, showed me the interior. It was definitely the perfect place for us.

He who hesitates is lost. Even I know that! My mind went into "The Art of the Deal" mode. The Donald Trump in me started to percolate. I remembered the shrewd negotiating techniques I'd learned long ago from Robert Allen's real estate classic, *Nothing Down*. Make an offer immediately; lock up the property; salt the offer with plenty of contingencies; bail if the seller isn't motivated enough.

I asked Shahri to pump the seller's broker for information.

- ✔ "What's the least the seller will take?"
- ✔ "How motivated is he?"
- ✔ "How quickly does he need to sell?"

Shahri warned me: "Bobby, this is a good deal already. Don't blow this by trying to make it a steal. You don't want to break Marti's heart, do you?" Ooh, I hate it when they try to be reasonable with me like that.

I called Marti to let her know I thought it was a "go". She was thrilled that I liked the place. Her one request was: "Honey, please don't get too tricky and negotiate us out of this deal. I REALLY want this place."

I was stuck between a rock and a hard place. Negotiating is in my blood — I'm trained to go for the jugular in a deal. Marti affectionately calls me the junkyard dog. I'm usually validated for my money-saving skills, but, now Shahri and Marti were tossing a wet blanket on the fire I felt raging inside of me in anticipation of the upcoming haggle-fest.

But then, it came out of nowhere. Like a bolt of lightning, it suddenly hit me. "It can't be, can it?" That sound, that sound I hate to hear, was shrieking into both my ears. It was — THE VOICE OF REASON.

Okay. I get it. My wife loves the place. My Realtor says don't blow it. It is a good deal. Interest rates are at a two-decade low. Just do it!

And I did. I offered the asking price. Ouch! It hurt!!! But, while the pain was just subsiding from its most intense point, the whole Gestalt changed. The offer came back accepted. Marti was ecstatic. Shahri was relieved. The seller was happy. It closed without a hitch. We moved right in and we're grateful every day that we live in the domicile of our dreams.

LESSON

Money is important, no doubt. Saving money is always a great feeling. More important though is domestic tranquility. Peace and harmony in a marriage have no price tag. Sometimes when something seems too good to be true, and it's just right for you . . . it might be the time not to negotiate.

"The best way to fill time is to waste it."

— Marguerite Duras

10

Power, Time and Information

(PTI) = Titanium Results

For rewards beyond your wildest dreams, let's look at the core concept of Herb Cohen's classic book: *You Can Negotiate Anything*. This master negotiator gives us the key for negotiation clout: learn how to use power, time, and information (PTI). Remember the tiny acronym, PTI, and you will attract titanium results.

My assistant (I'll call her Roxy) was severely injured. At first, Roxy tried to represent herself before the insurance company. Ultimately, she became frustrated and asked me to represent her. Roxy felt powerless; she had insufficient information and was wasting too much precious time. Knowing PTI comes to the rescue in understanding the dynamics of this personal injury claim.

Power

You see — Roxy has ultimate power. Yes, even against the gargantuan insurance company. She has the power to sign the RELEASE AND SETTLEMENT document. Her signature on this has big value to the company. Without admission of liability, it would put a ceiling on their monetary outlay. It would release them from any future claims. And, very importantly, it would stop their investment of any additional legal resources in "working" the claim.

Wonderful. Yet, there are two sides to every story. Roxy needs surgery. She needs it now; she is in pain.

So, you see — the insurance company has power too. They have the power to withhold funding her surgery until the settlement figure is to their liking. On the other hand, their power weakens, considering the "hazards of litigation". It costs big bucks to defend a claim. In a trial, the risk exists for a jury award far in excess of the settlement Roxy might take now.

Information

The more we learn about our insurer-opponent, the more ammo we have. The opposite is also true. Trying to sound concerned and feigning empathy, the agent initially extracted valuable information from Roxy. He asked about her finances, insurance, family and governmental resources. She tipped her hand. Now he knows. She's broke, has no insurance and has no family or governmental fallback position.

That's okay. We continued to assemble information about the company's position. At first, they would admit to only $5,000 being available without trial. With more prodding, we found that they really had no absolute cap on medical reimbursement.

Time

No matter what we personally want, we all have to pay the price with our time. Okay, we're willing to do that. But, there's a limit. As a wise man once said: "Time is a great teacher, but unfortunately, it kills all its pupils." Roxy can't afford to wait forever. She must continue to bear the pain while we negotiate.

Again, from the other perspective, there is pressure on the agent to close the case. Time has value to him and the company. They need to settle. We need to settle.

As I write this, the settlement is still pending. We continue to be patient; we want our opponent's expenditure of time to be great. I continue to personalize Roxy's situation to the agent so he will see her as an injured person and not just a number. I continue to gather information that will help Roxy get the maximum settlement. We know we have power. We won't sign until we know we're getting the most the company will possibly give. Conversely, we continue to convey the impression that we are not in a hurry; we can afford to wait until we get a proper settlement.

COHEN LESSON 1

"Be patient, be personal, be informed —
any of you can bargain successfully for anything."

COHEN LESSON 2

"Power is based upon perception —
if you think you've got it, then you've got it!"

"America is the only nation in history which miraculously has gone directly from barbarism to degeneraton without the usual interval of civilization."

— Georges Clemenceau

11

Be Nice

"Be Nice . . . Who's Your Boss?"
— Robert E. McKenzie, EA, Attorney

It is the charity event of the season. Each year, the "who's who" of our whole community turns out for the "Fur Ball," hosted by Pet Network, which helps find homes for lost and abandoned animals. Many of the local businesses donate to the silent auction.

A couple of years ago, my good pal, Bob P., bid on a package for himself and his lovely wife, Theresa — two nights at a nearby spa-resort/hotel-casino. Whoopee! He got it! They could hardly wait to exchange their certificate for a two-day mini-vacation.

Before Bob knew it, over a year passed. Uh-oh! The certificate expired. Undeterred, Bob made the reservations anyway. Armed with his superior negotiating skills and general bargaining bravado, he was confident he could work something out.

Check-in was smooth. Bob gave the desk clerk his certificate and left a credit card for incidentals. Nothing to it! He and his mate completely enjoyed their dual days of free fun.

Ah, but nothing lasts forever. Alas, time came to check out.

KA-THUD. It hit him like a ton of bricks! "I'm sorry, Mr. P., but the night auditor noticed your certificate expired several months ago. Should we just leave *all* the charges on your credit card, or, would you like to pay cash?" Ginny, the desk clerk, delivered the death knell.

Dauntless, Bob summoned his finely honed negotiation know-how. He remembered: "Be nice . . . who's your boss?" "Use the 'courtly language' that Bobby talks about."

"I understand, Ginny. You've got a tough job to do here. By the way, who here would have the authority to consider helping us on this?" Ginny smiled, thanked Bob for his understanding and returned quickly with her supervisor, Raymond. She had brought her boss up to speed on the situation. More importantly, it appeared she had told Raymond that Bob was a nice guy. Raymond was smiling. He extended his hand and introduced himself.

"I understand we have a little technical difficulty here with your certificate, Mr. P."

Now listen to how beautifully Bob handles closing the "sale".

"Hi, Raymond, great to meet you. I know how busy you must be and I really want you to know how very much I appreciate your investing a couple of moments of your valuable time with us. I'm just wondering, is there any chance you might be so kind as to consider extending us the courtesy, on a one-time basis, of honoring our certificate as a gesture of good faith and in the spirit of helping abandoned animals?"

"Mr. P., it would be our pleasure. I hope you enjoyed your stay with us."

"Thank-you so much, Raymond, and please thank Ginny for her helpfulness too. You can bet we'll be back and that we'll tell our friends about your graciousness."

LESSON 1

Be nice. Politeness is a social lubricant too often forgotten in the negotiation process. If lesson one doesn't work, see lesson two.

LESSON 2

Who's your boss? Asking the wrong person for a favor won't work. Only negotiate with the one who has the authority to "be so kind as to extend you the courtesy on a one-time basis of . . ." You know the rest!

GOLDEN RULE

Thank the person who does you a favor. Compliment their establishment. Recommend it to others. A very classy final touch is to send a thank-you card to your new friend *and* send a letter of commendation to his or her boss. Certainly they *will* remember you when you return. And, you *will* get extraordinary service from then on too!

"Money costs too much."

— Ross McDonald, *The Goodbye Look*

12

Motels: Moonlight Madness and Savings Galore

Back in '76, I worked as a desk clerk in a large motel in South Lake Tahoe, California. My boss gave me specific orders. If we had rooms left later in the evening, I was to sell them at a discount if necessary. As long as we got enough to cover maid service plus some small change, we were ready to entertain all offers. I had the liberty and the license to negotiate!

He told me to quote the regular (rack) rate first. Sometimes, the potential guests gagged on that and turned on their heels to look elsewhere for a better rate. That's when my negotiation duties began.

First, I was to check out their manner of dress, jewelry and, especially, what kind of car they drove. "Size 'em up — get a feel for the most you think they'll pay."

So, I'd call them back. "Say folks. It's starting to get late now. Let's see if we can't work something out here that will make you happy. What's the most you would be comfortable with for the room?" Usually their eyes would brighten, thrilled at the prospect of getting a deal without any moonlight shopping.

My boss taught me "the first one who mentions a number loses". Granted, I quoted the rack rate - yet, that doesn't really count. That's high retail. Consider the quoted rack rate to be only an interesting opening bargaining position on the motel's part.

Then our prospective guests would usually offer just a little under the rack rate. Unfortunately for them, that's much more than we would have taken. You might end up in this situation.

If it is late in the evening and you think there are rooms left, you might have a bargaining boon on your hands. Check out the parking lot. It you see lots of empty parking spaces, Lady Luck is probably smiling on you. Let's say the desk clerk quotes the rack rate of $69.99 plus tax.

A Practice Dialogue

You: FLINCH. "Wow. That's a lot" Now, just be quiet. Silence is deadly in negotiations. Let your words echo throughout the lobby. "That's a lot" "That's a lot" "That's . . .," etc. If the clerk doesn't voluntarily offer you a lower price, start to walk out. "I think we'll look around for a rate we can afford." Keep walking until the desk clerk calls you back.

Desk Clerk: (This may sound familiar.) "Say folks. It's starting to get late. Let's see if we can't work something out here that will make you happy. What's the most you would be comfortable with for the room?"

You: "What's the least you could let us have it for?"

Remember three things here:

- The first person who mentions a number loses,
- The person asking the questions controls the negotiation, and
- Don't accept without "nibbling" for a little something extra; otherwise, your opponent might think he could have gotten more from you.

Desk Clerk: "$59.99 plus tax is about the best I could do for you."

You: "That's still sounds like a lot. I think we'll keep looking unless you can help us a little more."

Desk Clerk: "Man, you're tough! Okay. $49.99 plus tax. But, that is the lowest."

You: "That still sounds high. But, since it is getting late we'd consider that rate if you'll throw in a continental breakfast."

Desk Clerk: "My boss isn't going to be thrilled about this. But, you seem like nice folks so . . . all right. Enjoy your stay and your breakfast. By the way, have you been reading Bobby Covic's book?"

"The optimist proclaims that we live in the best of all worlds and the pessimist fears that this is true."

— James Branch Cabell

13

Killer Keys to Hotel Savings

I was booked to speak at a convention in San Francisco and needed a reservation for three nights. Location: A big-name (chain) hotel. (Let's call it Hyarriott). I was being paid a flat fee. Any reduction on lodging was extra profit for me. I ended up saving BIG BUCKS!!! Read on . . .

Since the hotel is part of a chain, I checked their website. "Net" prices are often the lowest published. Result: "Cheapest" room — $269.

Next, I called their 800 number. Sara answered and quoted me the dreaded "rack rate" — $298. I was shocked! "Your website lists the same room for $269." Her confession followed, "Oh, that's the 'corporate' rate; I can extend you that price." (Plus 14.045% tax!)

I started to grind. "With tax, that's $306.78. That's way too much." I asked about specials, leisure rates and weekend rates. Nothing.

Next, I called the hotel reservations desk. Debra started at $298 and quickly dropped to $269 after I cited the 800 number experience. I knew I could do better.

Jumping into action. I tried 'em all: AAA, government,

frequent flyer, Hyarriott Gold Card. Forget it. I kept trying: specials, leisure rates, airline specials, weekend rates, special event rates. Still a bust.

Finally, I was onto something. "What about AARP?" (American Association of Retired Persons).

"Well, we had a small block of $125 rooms on an AARP special. Unfortunately, they're all sold out." Darn!

"There must be something you can do," I said. She checked the computer. "Well, we do have the regular AARP discount. That would be $242. Still way too rich for my blood. I liked the sound of $125.

Resort to Higher Authority

Never negotiate with a person who doesn't have the authority to give you what you want. I know that rule!

"Debra, do you have the authority to make an exception and extend me that $125 AARP block rate?" She didn't. I asked who did. She said nobody. I knew where to go — up the chain of command. I tried the rooms' manager. No luck. Next the manager of the day. No go. Finally, the hotel manager. I got his voice mail and asked for a return call.

Early the next morning his assistant, James, called me. He apologized that the manager wasn't available. I recited the magic words: "James, I am a Hyarriott Gold Card Member and frequent guest of your hotel chain. I'm wondering if you might be so kind as to consider extending me the courtesy on a one-time basis of making an exception and giving me the AARP $125 block rate."

He hemmed. He hawed. He told me it was a busy period, that he'd have a hard time justifying it. I remained silent. Finally, the ice melted. "Okay, Mr. Covic. I'll help you out. I'll transfer you to the front desk and tell them to book it."

Only $142.56 a night with the tax. From the rack rate, it *saved me $591.87* over three nights! Right to my bottom line.

Right into my pocket. You can bet a nice thank-you note was on its way to James. I praised his courtesy and professionalism. I even sent a copy to the manager.

LESSON

Check the hotel website, 800 number and reservations desk. Play them against one another. Flinch. Ask for discounts. Keep trying. Go up the chain of command if necessary and resort to higher authority. Never give up. Silence creates tension. Send a thank-you note.

Did I have to invest some time? Yes. Was it worth it? We both know the answer to that question!!!

> *"I feel closest to hell when I'm thinking about money."*
>
> — Pharoah Sanders

14

"No Money Down" Real Estate

Fact or Fiction?

Maybe you're worried about money. You can't sleep. You turn on the tube. There it is again. That same old infomercial. Those same happy faces. From all over the U.S. of A. — men and women of all races, shapes and sizes. Young, old, married, single. Wearing colorful Aloha wear, they testify from poolside at a luxury Hawaiian resort hotel. With religious-type fervor, they tell the same old stories. "If I can do it, you can, too!"

The blue Pacific rolls in the background, trade winds blow through the palms and the warm island sun illuminates the set. Their mentor interviews them.

"So Al, before you bought my super-duper audio cassette/ CD-ROM success program, what was your life like?"

"Well Carl, I was unemployed and my beautiful wife, Mary, here [hugs spouse] was a homemaker. We had three young children to raise. The rent was due. We were broke and desperate. We saw you on TV one night and, BINGO, we knew we had to give your system a try."

You know the rest. Neither of them had any real estate

experience. They just followed the simple step-by-step instructions. They were actually surprised by how easy it was.

Next, one by one, pictures of their 13 "no money down" real estate acquisitions flash past on your screen. In less than a year, Al and Mary's net worth skyrocketed to $1.6 million. Monthly cash flow: Over $5,000.

They love doing this; it's fun. They work together as a team. They can't thank Carl enough. Finally they have "quality time" together.

"Enough, already." You're still worried about money. Remote in hand, you start to end the late-night foolishness. This is ridiculous. It can't be for real!

Or, could it? You begin to wonder. You remember the "practical proverbs of your youth".

- ☛ If it sounds too good to be true, it probably is.
- ☛ You don't get something for nothing.
- ☛ Nothing is easy.

Okay. "But, what if?" Then you start playing "devil's advocate" with yourself.

- ☛ Nothing ventured — nothing gained.
- ☛ With a goal and hard work, you can make anything happen.
- ☛ There must be something to it.

"Forget it." You flip the channel to end the fantasy.

Fact or Fiction?

Probably a little of both, for sure. Let me share my experience with you. On a small scale, I did it. So, I know it is possible. Yes, I bought a rental house with no money down. I even got a little bit of cash when the escrow closed! I painted the interior, installed a used refrigerator, turned around and rented it out. Between the tax breaks and the rent, I did better than break even.

Reality Check

Was it easy? No. Did I have to invest a lot of time finding the "motivated seller"? Yes. Was it fun? No. Did I have years of property management headaches? Yes. Did it give me a wonderful opportunity to own an investment that my tenants' monthly rent checks paid for? Yes.

Conclusion

I'm sure some of the overnight sensation, instant millionaire, rags to riches success stories are true. On the other hand, and again — from my experience, refer to "practical proverbs of your youth" above. Sure, anything is possible. You gotta believe to succeed, no doubt. Yet remember, "With a goal and hard work, you can make anything happen." It's hard work, not easy money! At the end of the day, here's a good thing to keep in mind. The people who made the most money during the Gold Rush made it selling shovels to hopeful miners!

"Whenever choosing between the lesser of two evils, choose neither."

— Unknown

15

Crisis Negotiating

How Not to Do It

DATELINE Turlock, CA. Summer 1961. Beaming stadium lights, muggy August night, roaring crowd, freshly manicured grass. With my nifty, little, white-plastic ball and strike counter in my pocket, I finished my frosty A & W root beer and sauntered onto the diamond.

My buddy, Jimbo, was "the man in black" covering the field. I was the big man behind the plate. We were umpires for the Little League season.

Jets versus Pirates. The field was teeming with serious looking 7th graders. The stands were brimming with eager, excited and nervous parents.

On it went, smooth as Chinese silk, not a hitch. Jimbo and I were pros, running the game with mastery.

Moving into the latter innings; close score. Jets "up". Behind two runs, two "men" on and two outs — little Johnny Farley approaches the plate, the pressure is on.

First pitch: Swing and a miss. "Strike one!" Next pitch: high and outside. "Ball one!" Third pitch: right in there; he should've nailed it. "Strike two!" Two more pitches, both way out of the zone. "Ball two!" "Ball three!"

The tension mounted. It didn't faze me though; just another game. My mind wandered. I could see myself cruisin' home after the game, takin' it easy, watchin' a little boob tube and conkin' out on the couch.

Johnny swings and misses again. "Strike two!" I holler authoritatively.

And then . . . everything came to a screeching halt. Silence, confusion, then mania. "What's wrong with you ump; are you crazy?" The Pirate crowd was going berserk. "He's outta there!" "That was the third strike!" "Can't you count?"

I looked at Jimbo. His co-ump face telegraphed: RED ALERT!

Their faces flaming in anger, the Jets' parents were coming right towards me. My mind was blank. What happened?

Uh-oh. It finally hit me. Darn. I FORGOT. I *forgot* to turn the strike wheel on my counter. Oh no! I left the strike counter on "1" when I should have turned it to "2" after that perfect pitch Johnny should've nailed. That last miss was Johnny's third strike.

Crisis Negotiation: How Not to Do It

I panicked. At first I stuck to my guns. "Three and two — three balls, two strikes!" I held up my counter as evidence. Forget about that. They were coming at me like a lynch mob. There was only one way out. "Okay. Okay. I see what happened." My pride wasn't worth my life.

"Strike three. Batter you're outta there!" Relieved, I thought that would do the trick. The Jets' parents jeered me a little and started back to the stands. Next, the Pirates' families started in on me. They wanted little Johnny to have one more shot at it. "The *ump* said three and two. We're going with that."

Just what I needed. There I was smack dab in the middle. What to do? There was only one thing to do. I had to eat crow and I had to eat it fast. Time for humble pie dessert.

"I'm sorry. I made a mistake. Johnny's out. Three strikes. I'm sorry. I should've turned my counter. I didn't. I was wrong. Get back out there and play ball!"

LESSON

Admit it when you're wrong. Everybody makes mistakes. Hopefully, when you make your next one, it won't be in the middle of a large crowd with competing interests!

Call 'em like you see 'em. But, for heaven's sake, pay attention. Keep track of what's going on in life. When you're in charge, keep your eye on the ball and don't forget to "change the strike counter".

> *"When choosing between two evils, I always take the one I haven't tried before."*
>
> — Mae West

16

$3,600+ Per Hour?

Big Returns on Negotiating Skills

You get the opportunity almost every day! *You* get a chance every time you buy something. *You can make big bucks by saving big bucks.*

A wise old man by the name of Benjamin Franklin once counseled: "A penny saved is a penny earned." Makes sense to me. At the end of the day, funds less depleted are just as valuable as newly earned funds added to an existing stash. So, how much can *you* earn by saving? Lots! Believe me. Just wait 'til you see the math later in the example below.

Example

You've worked hard sharpening your bargaining and negotiating skills. Your car needs repair. Your local mechanic tells you to take your car to the dealership for a specialized job. Ouch! You know the pain of dealership bills — outrageous hourly labor rates and even more outrageous price tags on parts. Are you just gonna take it? No way! You get ready to join the ranks of the financially successful. You posture yourself for the challenge, and you go for it.

You introduce yourself to the service manager, Al. He looks the job up in "the book". He then cheerfully quotes you $178.60 in labor and $400 in parts. He awaits your response. You gag. You flinch. You use your logic — "labor, probably non-negotiable; parts, big mark-up, possibly negotiable. Worth a try."

"$400 in parts! Wow!! That's a lot!!!" Pause. "Al, what kind of discount could you extend me on the parts?"

Silence. More silence. Al rustles some papers. "15% is the best I can do for you, my friend." Trying to contain your glee, you thank Al for his graciousness in extending you this courtesy. You don't feel too sorry for the dealership. You guess their markup is easily 300%. Finally, you make a mental note to yourself to send Al a thank-you note when you get home.

Now, here's the math

15% x $400 = $60. Right? Right! That's fantastic!!! You just saved $60. Congratulations. And, the good news is that there isn't any bad news. It only gets better. Stay with me now.

Next, estimate how long it took you to gag, flinch and think — "labor, probably non-negotiable; parts, big mark-up, possibly negotiable. Worth a try." (30 seconds). Then, estimate how long it took you to say: "$400 in parts! Wow!! That's a lot!!!" (5 seconds). "Al, what kind of discount could you extend me on the parts?" (10 seconds). And, last, how long did you have to remain silent until Al gave you the discount? (15 seconds). Okay. Let's add all the seconds up. 30 + 5 + 10 + 15 = 60. You've heavily invested in this negotiation to the extent of 60 seconds of your precious time. One minute.

Test

You just saved $60 in one minute. There are 60 minutes in an hour. In this case, how much are your negotiating skills worth on an hourly basis? Well, how about $60 Saved X 60 Minutes =

$3,600. $3,600 AN HOUR? That's right. Pro-rated, that's the hourly value of your bargaining powers. Not bad.

Unless you're Bill Gates or Oprah Winfrey, I'm guessing that $3,600 an hour is more than you presently make. Am I right? That's what I thought.

Far-fetched? Maybe. Do the numbers work? You bet they do. Most people will never earn as much money working for an hour as they can save by negotiating effectively for one minute. And, the better you get at it, the more you'll save/earn because you'll keep applying your valuable skills to bigger and bigger ticket items.

> *"I've been on a calendar, but never on time."*
>
> — Marilyn Monroe

17

Late Check-Out

Free Rent for "Welcomed Guests"

You've seen it. I've seen it. We've all seen it. It's posted for all weary travelers and "welcomed guests" to see. On the inside doors of cheap motel rooms, more discreetly placed elsewhere in luxury hotel suites, on the walls behind the check-in counters, etc. It might be anywhere. Rest assured though, the ominous warning is posted. And, the message is clear: CHECKOUT TIME 11:00 AM.

True Story of the Day

It was mid-July, Washington, DC. I was speaking at the luxurious Hyarriott Hotel. Scheduled to speak 'til 2:40 pm on the last day of my stay, I had a 5 pm flight booked. The checkout time that worked for *me* was 3:15 pm. See how easy it can be.

Her: Hotel operator.

Me: May I have the front desk please?

Her: Hold for the front desk. *(Click, followed by the scratchy Muzak of a Neil Manilow jewel)*

(New) Her: Front desk. This is Phyllis.

Me: Hi, Phyllis! *(Establish rapport. Use employee's name).* Bobby Covic in 1854. *(Introduce yourself with authority. Identify your room number as if it were your home address. Imply your power: "You guys can't kick me out of my own room.")* You know, Phyllis, *(Employee's name)*, I'm a speaker *(Establish credibility)* with the NTPI *(Name recognition)* convention *(Big out-of-town dollars, blocks of rooms, banquets, etc.)* We *(We = the power of plurality. It's not just you alone)* have been with you *(Personalize with the word "you")* for five days *(Big out-of-town dollars, blocks of rooms, banquets, etc. — to the 5th power)* now. Phyllis *(Employee's name)*, I understand *(Empathy)* and appreciate *(Respect)* your usual *(Notwithstanding the exception I'm going to ask for)* checkout time is 11:00 am.

I hope you can help me. *(People like to help people)* I need *(not 'could you give me?')* an extended *(not a 'late')* check-out to 3:15 pm. *('Late' check-out admits to your tardiness. That allows their justification of additional charges.)*

I don't finish speaking until 2:40. I usually can't get out of the ballroom after questions until about 3. I can be packed and ready to go after that in about 15 minutes. *(Long-winded explanation. Phyllis has guests in line waiting to check out. Her stress level is rising.)*

Her: *(Resorting to the first level of house defense)* I can extend you to 2 without charge.

Not acceptable. I asked for 3:15. I want 3:15 and I want it with no extra charge. I know she can and will do it. It's a game. I keep playing.

Me: Phyllis, *(Employee's name)* may I speak to the Hotel Manager *(Highest authority)* please? *(Firm but polite).*

Her: I could connect you with the Rooms Manager *(Doesn't want to bother Hotel Manager).*

Me: Okay. *(Willing to compromise)* That would be great. *(Agreeable,* *pleasant, appreciative)* Thank-you. *(Polite) (Click, more scratchy Muzak - Kenny G. playing an Elton Diamond jewel).*

I wait. I know the drill. She'll never go to the trouble to find the Rooms Manager. She's way too busy. She comes back on the line.

Her: I'm going to just go ahead and extend you until 3:15.

Me: Thanks, Phyllis. I really appreciate your help.

LESSON

Checkout when YOU want. Even if you're not with a big convention, you can make this work. The 11:00 AM CHECKOUT ruse is an Artificial Time Crisis. Don't buy into it. Let 'em know you know the game. They'll quit playing before you will. You'll win. The right words to the right person in the right way will do it for you every time.

*"There are times when everything goes well;
don't be frightened; it won't last."*

— Jules Renard

18

The Turn of a Phrase

It's Not WHAT You Say; It's HOW You Say It

Sometimes the perfect words just seem to roll off our tongues. This phenomenon is called: "the turn of a phrase". It's not *what* we say; it's *how* we say it. Though we frequently underestimate our linguistic talents, our periodic easy eloquence often takes us by complete surprise.

Here are three examples.

Scenario One

I'm in the video store. I pick out two videos. I'm on my way to the counter. I notice a box of used CDs marked $2.98. Much to my surprise, I find three I like. I don't want to pay $8.94 plus tax. Besides, the shrink-wrap on one of them is torn.

- ☛ ***Phrase***: "These are used. How 'bout three for six bucks?"
- ☛ ***Response***: "Okay, I can do that."

Analysis: KISS. Keep it simple, Sparky! I smiled, made eye contact and implied that, since they were "used", they were worth even less than the marked $2.98. I fingered the ripped shrink-wrap. I "asked" but actually conveyed the attitude of assumption. I used round numbers. I used slang my Generation Next clerk could relate to: "How 'bout" and "six bucks". Then, I just kept quiet and awaited his assent. Simple, short, slang, silence.

Scenario Two

It's almost closing time; I'm in a hotel gift shop. I go to the counter with my sage selections of junky late night snacks. I spot a box of Ghirardelli chocolate squares located right next to the register. No way do I want to pay whatever the inflated "impulse item" price is for one of these yummy treats. Yet, I crave the chocolate and love the challenge.

> ☛ ***Phrase:*** "How 'bout throwin' in one of these since I'm such a good customer?"
>
> ☛ ***Response:*** "Okay."

Analysis: Again, simple is the key. AFTER the clerk had rung up my other items, he began depositing them into a plastic bag. Then, I made my move, and turned the phrase. I picked up the chocolate square and, in slow motion, began a movement towards the open bag. Simultaneously, I "asked". By the time the words were out of my mouth, the chocolate was in the bag. As it klunked into the bottom of the bag, the clerk approved. The non-verbal message I transmitted was that I (not only deserved, but) already "owned" the treat. Simple, slow, smooth, self-assured.

Scenario Three

I'm in the supermarket with my wife. I'm paying for the

goodies. My wife comes running up with a last-minute necessity — a single ice cream sandwich. Perplexed, yet with some indecision, the checker asserts she can't scan it since it is out of the box and has no bar code. My wife is disappointed. The clerk reaches for the sugary delight and tentatively announces she will have to restock it. My wife's disappointment turns to grief.

- ☛ ***Phrase:*** "Fifty cents!" I exclaim. (As I nod my head up and down in "yes" mode.)
- ☛ ***Response:*** Cha-ching! (The electronic version anyway).

Analysis: I immediately resolved the clerk's problem. Initially, she was perplexed, indecisive and tentative. I bailed her out with absolute resolve and supreme certainty. I turned the phrase. Then, in one continuous motion, I pulled two quarters out of my pocket (implying a request for her extended hand) and dropped the coins graciously into her upturned palm. The deal was sealed.

LESSON

Little by little you can save a lot. Learn to turn a phrase on a moment's notice. Keep it simple, short and smooth. Exude confidence; nod your head. Most importantly though, remember to thank the nice person who responded so positively to the phrase you turned.

Solipsism:

n., an appealing theory that the self is the only reality — especially popular among philosophers and winners.

— Loosely attributed to Coco Pekelis, Author
Everything I Know I Learned on Acid

19

"It's Not My Policy . . ."

The Setup for the Simple Close

Hotels have policies. Guests pay bills. That's the way the game is set up — a very subtle form of intimidation. Here's a true story to show you how to set your own policy and turn the tables on a hotel, or any kind of business that has the apparent power to make the rules.

These days, many business travelers go online with their laptops through a local prefix. Major hotel chains are now using this as a convenient excuse to assert "per minute" charges for local calls and to line their pockets at the expense of their uninformed and unsuspecting guests.

Going way back, I had a hard time swallowing the 50-cent flat fee for a local call. Then it was 75-cent flat, next 80 . . . and now this. I don't like getting nickeled and dimed by a hotel any more than I would like getting nibbled to death by ducks. (Interestingly enough, both use bills to attack!)

I make it a habit to always ask for a "draft" of my hotel bill prior to checkout. This allows me to spot any silliness of the "per minute" sort and develop a money-saving strategy.

A Hyarriott tried this new trick on me recently. Now, if they had told me when I checked in, I might have knuckled under and eaten the charges. If they had a sign by the phone — yeah, sure, I would have probably kept my online time short and paid the piper. But, so sorry, Charlie, I didn't like the surprise charges on the "draft" of my bill.

I asked who had the authority to make an adjustment on my bill. Shortly, I was talking to "The Man". Walter, the Front Desk Manager, asked how he could be of service. I gave him my business card to establish my credibility. I explained that I was a member of the *Hyarriott Gold Rewards Club*. This further confirmed my "posture power". Asked if he'd like to see my membership card, he politely declined assuring me that he trusted me. I mentioned that I was a frequent guest at Hyarriott. This affixed in his mind my value as an ongoing source of revenue.

See how the set-up works? I gave him reasons in advance to justify saying yes to my (as yet unknown) request. I quickly conveyed credibility, posture power and value. I elicited a confirmation of his trust in me.

I deferred to him politely as the man in charge. The message I subconsciously conveyed was that he could grant my request and still feel good about himself. He could say yes with his self-esteem still intact.

I was calm and expressed no anger. I spoke quietly. I employed the age-old and non-threatening negotiating classic: "I don't understand. Can you help me?" *(Remember the television detective Columbo?)* I simply asked for an explanation of the phone charges.

He offered the explanation I expected. By indicating my understanding, I validated his communication skills. This put us on the same side. We were partners preparing in tandem to address my discomfort with the "draft" of the bill.

I closed with simplicity. *"It's not my policy* to pay more than the base rate for local calls." Walter conceded gracefully, adjusted the bill and bid good day to another happy guest.

LESSON

Think about what actually won the adjustment — thoughtfulness, a plan, preparation, proper set-up and a simple close. These are the how-to keys for ensuring that *your "policy"* dictates the debit to your credit card and not the hidden, secret and silly policy of the hotel.

"Walk softly and carry a big stick."

— Teddy Roosevelt (I think!)

20

Effective Complaining

Don't Get Mad — Get "Adjusted"

I had chronic problems with the phone in my room at a major Las Vegas hotel. Long story short: The problems severely diminished my ability to communicate efficiently with my wife. The telephonic difficulties didn't do much to facilitate a sustained state of marital bliss during my visit to Glitter Gulch.

Situation

I had a legitimate complaint. I complained effectively. Result: Bill adjusted by 50% of one night's lodging. With tax, the savings to me were $56.37. I felt that was reasonable under the circumstances. The lost revenue to the hotel was certainly worth the goodwill created. To prove it — ask me about the hotel. I'll tell you good things!

Here's the story. Upon checkout, I obtained a "draft" of my bill. I asked who had the authority to make an adjustment. I was referred to Elliot, the assistant manager. I had a goal. I wanted an adjustment to my bill commensurate with the inconvenience.

As I waited, I observed Elliot being harangued by a very angry woman guest. She made demands. He resisted. Her tirade intensified and merely reinforced his resolve to resist. Finally she left in a huff.

During their discourse, I reflected on my strategy. I planned to present Elliot with an opportunity — not a confrontation. I planned to explain my problem and to offer an opportunity for Elliot to right a wrong.

The Sandwich

I prefaced and concluded my complaint with a compliment. I kept the complaint itself constructive and concise. I offered a solution.

"Elliot, I want you to know I've really enjoyed my stay with you here. Also, I'd like to compliment you on the way you just handled yourself with that angry woman. Anyway, I thought you would probably like to know about the discomfort I experienced in my marriage as a result of some problems with the phone in my room." *[Problems explained.]* "I would feel a lot better about things if you would consider making an adjustment to my bill. Again, please know I think you're running a first-class operation here and I realize that things can't always be perfect."

Anger

Remember: Think opportunity, not confrontation. Anger has no place in delivering an effective complaint. I didn't raise my voice. A whisper is more productive than a roar. I consciously lowered my voice when I asked for the adjustment. This displayed my respect for Elliot. It symbolized my taking him into my confidence.

Threats

Reminder: Walk softly and carry a big stick. Threats aren't appropriate in the context of a complaint. A positive approach works better. Implying that you'd prefer not to have to do something is more powerful than actually threatening to do it. Alluding to pursuing alternative avenues of redress is more effective than saying you're going to sue. I knew no "implying" or "alluding" would be necessary with Elliot. He was a gentleman, a professional, and an astute manager.

Conclusion

Elliot apologized on behalf of the hotel. He asked if I'd be comfortable with his proposed adjustment. I said most definitely, we shook hands and I went on my merry way — another satisfied guest.

LESSON

Customers actually do a business a favor by complaining. Studies reveal that on average only 35% of disgruntled customers actually complain. The other patrons with a beef just walk. A dissatisfied customer will rant, rave and rage about his negative experiences to between seven and nine would-be customers. Negative comments make twice the impact as positive comments. Complaining effectively benefits the business while allowing you to assert your concerns in an appropriate manner. Think opportunity — not confrontation.

"Mistakes are almost always of a sacred nature.
Never try to correct them."

— Salvador Dali, *Diary of a Mad Genius*

21

If It Sounds Too Good to Be True . . .

Knowing When Not to Negotiate

I still feel foolish. I'm still embarrassed. And, I could just kick myself for not having better sense.

Oh well. It happened over ten years ago — bygones and all that. Nevertheless, the story still begs to be told. So, for you, here's the shameful scoop.

The older condos I had my eye on were bound to be good investments. They were the least expensive entry-level condos in our big demand/low supply village. If not in the short-term, certainly over time these sleepers were destined to be big winners. The key was, as always, buying one at the right price.

I heard a friend's father (let's call him Larry) wanted to sell his unit. I called to feel him out. He "felt" $60,000 ($60K) was a "fair" price and expressed he was "firm". I knew $60K was a *very* solid bargain. Comparable units: $65 to $75K. The price was already $5K to $15K under market. I smelled blood.

I asked for a meeting. Larry agreed, but with a condition. If I were serious, I would prepare a written offer to present to him. I still smelled blood.

How much could I get him down? I started doing my homework.

My snooping indicated Larry was the classic motivated seller. Larry's son was living in the unit rent-free, abusing drugs and wrecking the place. The kid was probably breaking his father's heart. The old man probably couldn't bear the thought of evicting his own flesh and blood. Selling was a logical solution to an emotional problem.

I put together a cheesy low-ball offer with loads of contingencies. I rationalized. My strategy: If I was going to "steal" the property, $50,000 was a good opening position.

We met. I presented my offer. Larry was incensed, insulted and (I later figured out) injured on a very deep emotional level. At a very vulnerable time, he perceived that I was scheming to take unfair advantage of him. Sadly, my approach was ridiculously transparent and his perception was absolutely accurate.

I called to apologize and suggest we start over. It was too late. The damage was done. "You're not serious" were the last words I heard before he hung up.

I really blew it. Me, Mr. big-time, fancy-pants, savvy negotiator. I was deeply saddened to have to acknowledge that my opportunistic, cavalier and mercenary "strategy" cost me a great deal.

Don't Look a Gift Horse in the Mouth

There are times when you ought to simply pay a person the price asked — no questions asked.

Remember

Pigs get fat. Hogs get slaughtered. Leave a little on the plate for the other guy. Utilize understanding, empathy and compassion.

Give yourself a break too. There's always another day and another deal. Don't forget to listen with your heart — not just your ears.

Update

That condo I didn't want to break loose with $60K for? Present value: about $225K.

If only . . .

LESSON

If it sounds too good to be true it might not be too good to be true. It might be an honest to goodness gift of a deal staring you in the face.

The clues I disregarded at the time were Larry's three words: "felt", "fair" and "firm". He said he "felt" $60K was a "fair" price and he was "firm". I was totally insensitive to what was important to him on a *feeling* level. Regretfully, I was not concerned in the least about his sentiments, but only with my own greed.

"You can't get there from here."

— Firesign Theatre Comedy Troupe

22

Negotiating with Momentum

Motion: The Magic Potion

Every negotiation starts from a standstill. As in physics, the law of inertia controls. A body at rest tends to stay at rest; a body in motion tends to stay in motion. Example: a locomotive. Standing still, its tendency is to keep standing still. Once moving at full speed, its motion takes on a life of its own. The loco barrels along — defying interference with its cumulative energy.

Momentum in negotiating is the same. You must consciously and incrementally move the process from inertia to the critical mass of "Yes".

A True Story

Bob, and wife, T, were staying in San Francisco for a few days. Shopping was the agenda. Eventually, they found a fascinating Chinese antique shop. T was powerfully attracted to an incredible sculpture displayed in a magnificent glass case. Price: $520.

Negotiating is a game to my friends. Here are the techniques they won by.

Express Only Casual Interest

T knows to avoid showing excitement. She gives Bob a subtle

nudge but displays overtly only a mild curiosity. The nudge signals to Bob: Let the game begin.

Destroy Any Expectation Of A Large Profit In The Seller's Mind.

Making sure the owner can hear their patter; Bob acknowledges T's interest.

Bob: Honey, that's nice but we don't really need it. Besides, look at the price.

T: You're right dear, we don't. Wow! That price can't be right, can it?

Bob: Can't be.

Nevertheless, playing the doting husband, Bob tells T he'll ask the owner just for kicks.

The Initial ("It Can't Be True") Inquiry

Bob asks the owner if the amount could possibly be correct. Affirmative. Bob and T shrug, look around a little more and leave.

The Subsequent Inquiry

The couple returns the next day. The momentum begins to build.

Bob: You know, we're kind of interested in that piece. Is there tax on that too?

Owner: Yes. You pay tax, he said in his endearing Chinese dialect.

Bob: How much is the tax?

Owner: Tax, 8%.

Bob: How much is the total with the tax?

Owner: That total $586.43.

Bob: $586.43! *[Flinch]*. It's too much!!! *(This phrase blames* *the item, not the merchant. It insinuates Bob just can't afford it.)*

Bob: *[Complete silence] [Momentum stops].*

Owner: It nice piece, lovely. *[Momentum starts again].*

How Much If I Pay Cash?

Bob: If I pay you all in cash, how about $420. *[Momentum increases].*

"Cash" is a magic word in our society. To the owner, it implies avoidance of the two usual, and less desirable, alternatives: credit card *(transaction fee)* or personal check *(bouncy, bouncy).* To many merchants, cash suggests avoidance of paperwork and *(more importantly though less legally)* taxes. Cash allows a merchant to justify selling for a lower price.

Owner: Okay — $420 cash.

Bob: Okay. That's the total price now. You won't have to do any paperwork. So, no tax, right?

Owner: Right. Okay. That total. No tax.

Nibbling

Once the momentum is at this level, the owner is very susceptible to "nibbling". Nibbling is a tactic whereby buyer gets seller to agree to a set price and then uses the assumptive approach to get a few no-charge extras.

Bob: That does include packing and shipping too — doesn't it?

Owner: Well, okay. Usually extra charge. I do for you though. You good customer. What address you want shipped to?

Bob: *[Gives address]* How about throwing in a couple of boxes of incense with that too?

Owner: Oh, you such good bargainer. Okay. Incense no-charge. Where you learn to do that?

LESSON

Contain excitement. Destroy profit expectations. Multiple inquiries. Offer cash. Nibble. Take your time. Engage the seller. Create momentum. Motion is the magic potion.

23

Conquering the Convention Rate

Persistence, Policy and Patience Prevail

Here's a true story about how to conquer the hotel "convention rate." As always, creativity, persistence and audacity are a must.

Set-Up

I needed five night's lodging for a convention in our nation's capital. I called the DC Hyarriott where the convention was being held.

I got the usual: "Are you coming in with a convention?" Well, I know the opportunistic hotel industry sets the "convention rate" higher than the "regular rate" for the same room. So, wanting to avoid the dreaded and draconian "convention rate", I tested the waters.

Me: I'm traveling on my own. (True statement).

Them: I'm sorry, sir, we don't have any rooms available. We blocked almost all our rooms for a convention on the dates you're requesting.

Me: Okay. Thanks.

Me: (Calling back). I'd like to book five nights for the XYZ convention.

Them: We can offer you a special convention rate of $145 per night plus tax.

Me: Great. I'll take it.

The usual credit card conversation ensued. I got my confirmation number. I was all set. I resigned myself to $145 a night (plus tax) and considered it a closed case. But watch what happened.

Scenario — DC Hyarriott

I waited in line to check in. Shortly, it was my turn: "Covic (C O V I C), five nights." Julie, the desk clerk, was very pleasant and efficient. We joked as she scrambled around taking the obligatory imprint of my plastic, getting my key, etc. I just happened to look over the counter. I could see all my information on her computer screen. The $145 room rate literally jumped out at me. Like a blinding flash of lightning it hit me. "Give it a shot." I told myself. "You've got nothing to lose." Oh sure, I could embarrass myself a little. But that's just fodder for a little check-in levity anyway.

The First Act

Me*:* Julie, I'm Bobby Covic. *(Personalization)*

Me: Here's my business card. *(Legitimacy)*

Me: Also, Julie, I'm a Hyarriott Gold Rewards Member. *(Credibility and . . . this implies some kind of entitlement. I've set up an exception in Julie's mind now that I'm going to ask for something.)*

The Second Act

Me: *(Acting shocked)* Julie, your computer has my rate at $145 a night?

Her: Yes. $145 a night plus tax for five nights. That's the XYZ convention rate.

Me: *(Setting up the close — establishing loyalty)* Julie, you know I stay in Hyarriotts a lot.

The Third Act

Me: *(Delivering the close)* It's not my policy to pay more than $99 per night for lodging.

Me: *(Absolute silence)*

Me: *(Waiting patiently and expressing positive expectation)*

Her: We do have an AARP rate of $99 per night.

Me: That would be fine.

Her: Okay, Mr. Covic. Here's your key. Have a nice stay.

Me: *(Gracing her palm with a five-spot)* Thanks Julie. You've been great to work with! *(Appreciation and validation)*

The Winning Phrase

"It's not my policy to pay more than $99 per night for lodging."

Icing on the Cake

Guess what? To my surprise, Julie expressed her appreciation for my kindness, the tip and my positive comments on the Guest Comments card. On my final bill, she lowered my rate all the way down to $90! $55 saved per night X 5 nights = a $275 (plus tax) savings — Another Bargaining Windfall. Thanks, Julie!!!

LESSON

Be observant, creative and audacious. Be nice and use humor. Personalize. Create credibility and legitimacy. Express shock. Establish loyalty, state your policy and remain silent. Be patient, persistent and convey your positive expectation. Reward deserving people.

24

The Terror of "Touchy Feely"

You Gotta Find Their Soft Spot

Scenario

My car's air suspension pump died. My poor bruised butt became the last functioning part of my ride's previously smooth and sophisticated shock absorption system.

Dealership quote: Over $400. I knew there had to be a cheaper way.

Ironically, I had only recently junked my old car with Red Light Auto Dismantlers. It was the same year, make and model as my "new" one. Bingo! Since I actually gave them my worn-out hotrod, I figured the boys down at the "yard" would be glad to hear from me. So, expecting the royal treatment, I gave 'em a buzz.

Them: Red Light.

Me: Hi, Bobby Covic here. I gave you guys my old '89 Subaru XT-6 and I'm wondering if you could pull the air suspension pump off it and FedEx it up to me. I'm hoping you can just give it to me as a courtesy.

Them: ("Talk radio" crackling loud in the background) Who?

Me: (Repeat of the foregoing.)

Them: We ain't gonna just give it to 'ya.

Me: Who am I speaking with?

Them: This is Nolan.

Me: Nolan, are you the owner?

Them: No. Dean's the owner.

Me: Could I speak with Dean please?

Them: Hold on.

Them: This is Dean.

Me: (Repeat of the foregoing.)

Them: Yeah, okay. I'll put you back on to Nolan.

Them: (Nolan) Yeah.

Me: Nolan, Dean said I could have it. Could I get you to pull it and FedEx it up to me?

Them: We don't know nuthin' about any FedEx but you can come down and pull it out any time you want.

Me: Nolan, I don't know exactly how to explain this. I'm not too handy with tools. I'd need someone down there to actually pull it out for me.

Them: Well, okay, but most people pull the parts themselves. I can put you on the list and I'll get to it when I can.

Me: Great. When would be a good time for me to call

you back?

Them: I don't know. We're really behind right now.

Me: I understand. How about I call you around this time tomorrow?

Them: You can try.

Me: *(Next day and each subsequent day around the same time for over a week).* Hi Nolan, Bobby Covic here...

Them: *(More of the same evasive and non-committal responses.)*

Okay. You get the drift, huh? This was going nowhere fast. A creative change in approach was desperately needed. Here's how I turned it around.

Phrase

Me: Nolan, can we be really honest with one another?

Response: *(Silence)* What do you mean?

Phrase: Nolan, could you share with me if I've hurt your feelings or offended you in some way?

Response: Nah. It ain't nuthin' like that. Like I say, we just been real busy down here. I gotta coupla extra guys comin' in today. I'll see what I can do. Gimme a call back a little later.

Guess what? Within 45 minutes my phone rang.

Them: Bobby, this is Nolan. We got that part for 'ya. You can come down any time now.

Analysis

I could still be calling Nolan about that part. What happened? I simply changed the dynamic. I quit begging. After I gave up on the FedEx request, I tried the "touchy feely" approach. Apparently, my broaching the subject of Nolan's feelings created sufficient discomfort to change his whole demeanor.

LESSON

Insanity — Doing the same thing repeatedly and expecting a different result. This is especially true in negotiating. If one thing isn't working — try something different. The terror of the "touchy feely" approach might just make your opponent uncomfortable enough to get you what you want.

25

The Power of Personalization

The Cat's Meow

Picture this. Two equally competent legal professionals make separate written requests for an updated IRS document. (Exciting, huh?) One gets shoddy treatment. The other gets the kind of service usually reserved for the aristocracy.

- ☛ Question: Why the difference?
- ☛ Answer: Personalization.

Scenario

The first pro was my friend, Morgan, a well-respected author, speaker and trial lawyer. I was the second and, frankly, my credentials aren't as lofty. Nevertheless, I know how to use psychology to get what I want. Watch what worked for whom.

In early 2000, we each wrote to Washington, DC. Morgan received a dry reply indicating the current (1999) version of the document was not available to the public at that time. He ended up with a 1998 version.

I, on the other hand, received a cheery and very personable response along with the most up-to-date (1999) version.

Why?

Well, now this might sound a little silly, but — the only difference between Morgan's request and mine was my inclusion of one simple thing. That one small thing reached out and grabbed the attention of the processor. It distinguished my request from the thousands of impersonally dull, boring and ordinary ones. Before I reveal my silly little success secret, here's the background.

The Set Up

Seven years ago, I adopted an incredibly unique but very nameless red tabby-cat for my office. Initially traumatized, he meowed incessantly with a loud, plaintive and almost bellowing cry. "Malll, malll, malll." My secretary suggested he was telling us his name was Mel. We wanted to honor Mel with a name befitting the legal endeavors of our office — Mel soon morphed into Melvin. Finally, in a nod to infamous San Francisco attorney, Melvin Belli, we incorporated Mel's "bellow" into his moniker and ultimately christened him Melvin Bellows, Esq. Dignity now having been properly bestowed — all agreed the name fit.

Now, lest you think I've totally lost my mind and gone off on a totally irrelevant tangent, let me assure you — I' m still on track. Hang with me.

As time went by, my love for that little guy grew. Our hearts were inexorably connected. We communicated on the deepest level imaginable. Our mutual affection was immediately apparent.

Thankfully, the very visible bond that linked us was captured for posterity on film. A seriously soulful local photographer snapped the shot at a benefit for homeless animals. The brilliant colors immortalized the affinity — me holding Mel to my heart and Mel mugging for the camera — truly a match made in heaven.

But, what does all this have to do with personalization and getting what you want?

The Secret

Here's how I got what Morgan didn't. I simply included a print of that poignant photo in my request. Though Mel's presence now graces the big tax office in the sky, I'm eternally grateful that his majestic memory lives on so vividly in that magnificent photo. I almost always get what I want when I include Mel's image with a letter. Complete strangers everywhere continue to respond with uncharacteristic glee.

As long as I still have my prized negative, I'll keep a big stack of those photos of that fantastic feline and me in my drawer. One always goes out with each letter I send to anyone I don't know. When they see it, through Mel, they know me. I become a real person in their life. Real people get real responses and reasonable results. Personalize yourself in the eyes and hands of others and be ready for powerfully positive reactions.

LESSON

Personalize yourself. It helps when you put a face with your name. Avoid otherwise impersonal communications.

> *"Nobody can be exactly like me. Sometimes I even have trouble doing it."*
>
> — Tallulah Bankhead

26

How Do I Find out More?

Exceptional Books for Sharper Skills!

You Mean I Have to Read a Book? Well, no. You don't *have* to — that is *unless* you want to be more successful in life. Reading is a magic key to open the doors that stand between you and getting what you want. The American Indians have a saying: "When a man dies, a library burns down." Hopefully, when your number is up, you will have acquired (by reading) the kind of wisdom referred to by our original citizens. Wisdom leads to winning, and is yours for the taking from the pages of books.

You are already sharpening your negotiating skills each time you read a story in this book. Certainly, you are keen enough to know that I'm not just genetically blessed with unlimited cosmic access to all these shining nuggets of bargaining sagacity. I learned them the old-fashioned way. I read books and applied the knowledge offered — direct experience expands wisdom. Here are a few reference sources that will help you.

How to Win Friends and Influence People by Dale Carnegie

Originally written in 1936, this classic is the "bible" of human relations. A true masterpiece, it still sells big-time yearly. This is the unequaled primer on getting along with and influencing people. Carnegie's guide shows you:

- Easy ways to make people like you.
- The secrets of winning other folks over to your way of thinking.
- How to sell your ideas, constructively field complaints and avoid arguments.
- How to create enthusiasm for your ideas.
- Keep your relationships smooth and gratifying.

You Can Negotiate Anything by Herb Cohen

Master negotiator Cohen shares his winning experiences. He explains how to:

- Use power, information and time to your advantage.
- Understand the power of legitimacy, the artificial time crisis and the ploy of resorting to higher authority.
- Negotiate for mutual satisfaction.
- Win with Win-Win techniques.

This inexpensive little paperback still sells strong after decades of directing pros and neophytes alike.

Getting to Yes — Negotiating Agreement Without Giving In by Roger Fisher and William Ury

This national bestseller delivers insights from the Harvard Negotiation Project. It shows you how to:

- Separate the people from the problem.

- Focus on interests, not positions.
- Work together to create options that will satisfy both parties.
- Negotiate successfully with people who are more powerful, refuse to play by the rules or resort to "dirty tricks".

How to Argue and Win Every Time by Gerry Spence

Celebrity trial lawyer Spence shows you how to:

- Disarm an opponent by listening to the other side of the argument.
- Realize that words are often weapons of combat.
- Decide when to argue and when not to argue.
- Embrace the soul and argue out of the heart zone.
- Unlock the internal prisoner that prevents you from achieving victory.

Winning through Intimidation by Robert Ringer

Outrageous. You won't be able to put this one down. This business gem explains in candid terms:

- What intimidation is.
- How to avoid coming out on the short end of the stick.
- How to take the initiative in every area of your life.
- Why you become intimidated.

- How you can avoid the mental lapses that can cause you to fall victim to intimidation.

Okay, gang. There are five Jim Dandys for you. Let's get those pages turning. I give you my personal assurance that empowerment is yours for the taking. You'll make better bargains and get more bananas for your bucks as you master the ideas in these books!

27

Better Bargains for the Timid

Question

How can I avoid being timid and negotiate a better price at a garage sale even if the item is already a great buy? Mark Pilarski, Traverse City, MI

Answer

GREAT question Mark! I see three important elements here. Let's break them down.

How can you avoid being timid?

The word timid lives in the middle of in*timid*ation. To intimidate means to subdue, frighten, browbeat, coerce, extort, terrorize or scare. Pretty strong stuff, huh?

To avoid being timid, first acknowledge your tendency to be timid. Most of us feel timid — at least once in a while. At times we all feel shy, fearful, even fainthearted. Yet, we all know the gold goes to the gutsy.

That said, you've definitely got the right idea, Mark. Avoid transmitting a lack of courage. Dogs bite scared people.
Send a signal of confidence. Picture yourself proceeding fearlessly and courageously. *Be bold.*

Maintaining an erect stance will project a posture of power. Positive self-talk will help you. Repeat these affirmations to yourself:

"I am courageous."

"I am brave."

"I am fearless, daring and confident."

A smile will often disarm and confuse your opponent. Humor always helps break the tension and puts you in control.

*How can you negotiate a better price?

Well, Mark, you get a better price by asking for one. Don't ask — don't get! You maintain control by asking questions.

"How much were you hoping to get for this?"

"How flexible are you on that price?"

"What's the least you would be comfortable with?"

Convey an interest in the seller's feelings. Let the seller know you are concerned that he/she will feel okay about the deal.

What if the item is already a great buy?

Oh, this is where it really gets good. If the object of your desire is a steal at "list" price, you have an interesting challenge. Don't appear to be overly anxious. An image of mild curiosity and qualified interest will help. Be honest. Here are some comments you might make to the seller:

"I might be interested in buying this little gizmo." (Qualified interest)

"It looks like you've tried to price it realistically." (Honesty)

"My problem is, I'm on a pretty tight budget these days." (Not too anxious to part with your money)

"Maybe you could help me with some advice. I would like to make you an offer but I wouldn't want to insult you. Could I go ahead and let you know what I might be able to justify?"

You're letting the seller know that you really are a good guy, that you're short on dough and that you don't want him/her to feel taken advantage of. You don't want to come across as a brash brute that is insensitive and just making a low-ball offer.

LESSON ONE

Avoid appearing timid even if you feel timid. Be aware of intimidation tactics your opponent might be using. Don't fall for them. Convince yourself of your own confidence with positive visualization and affirmative self-talk.

LESSON TWO

Memorize phrases that will lead the seller to the amount you want to pay. Always appear that you are prepared to walk away if you don't get the bargain price you want. Let the seller know that you are just browsing and would consider buying only if the deal was attractive enough to you.

LESSON THREE

Remember, you're selling your money. Money is the monarch in the transaction. The seller can spend your money. You can't spend her gizmo.

Happy bargaining, Mark, and . . . thanks for the great questions!

28

Success: Any Questions?

"Life is a fragile bargain,
rescindable at any time by the other party."

— Joseph Epstein

Life is too short to wait very long for success. No question about it! Yet how to succeed? That's the question! Exactly what is the recipe for success? Glad you asked.

Ron Gilbert, Ph.D., Editor, *Bits & Pieces,* offers "The Four Surefire Rules for Success":

1. **Show up.**
2. **Pay attention.**
3. **Ask questions.**
4. **Don't quit.**

That sums it up pretty well, wouldn't you say? Check out # 3 above in Ron's Rules though. Ask questions. Think about it. Have you ever noticed the people you buy big-ticket items from ask a lot of questions? Example: Realtor selling you a house.

"What would be a comfortable down payment for you?"

"What kind of monthly payment would fit with your budget?"

"When would you like to move in?"

Well, it is not just that the realtor is a curious kind of person with an unusually strong personal interest in you. It is that he or she understands that we have *two* ears and *one* mouth for good reason. We're supposed to listen twice as much as we're supposed to talk. Easy to do if you ask questions. The one who asks questions in the transactions of life usually gains the desired outcome. Ask questions and listen.

The grandfather of motivation, Zig Ziglar, reminds us that: "You can get everything in life you want if you help enough other people get what they want." Discovery is the key.

Keep asking questions. Keep listening. Don't quit. Find out what other people really want. It is vital that you know what is important to them and why. When you identify their reasons behind what they want, you get access to their emotional "hot buttons".

This empowers you to tailor your negotiations to better satisfy their desires and, at the same time, get what you want. Be creative and devise win-win ways to help others attain their goals. Questions. Questions. Questions.

My friend, Bob P., asked me a couple of questions after he read my first few stories: "Where does the word 'negotiate' come from? And, what's the difference between negotiating and bargaining?"

Here's my answer. In Latin, the term *negotium* is made up of the syllables *neg* (not) and *otium* (ease). So, the English translation is, loosely, "not at ease." It implies a lack of settlement of terms, and invites the resolution of an agreement.

My goal is to help you get comfortable and be "at ease" negotiating.

As for Bob's second question, *Webster's* and *Wordfinder* define "negotiate" and "bargain" like this.

Negotiate: Argue, barter, dicker, haggle, work out, wrangle.

Bargain: Deal, exchange, swap, trade.

We negotiate to get a bargain. A bargain is a buy, a deal, a discount, a reduction. A bargain is something we get on sale, at a special price. We hope our bargain is a real deal.

While we are enjoying the gift of life, we might as well make it as fruitful as possible. A key to success in anything is the ability to negotiate. Be clear on what you want; discover what the other person wants — what their "hot buttons" are. Find a way to make it work using those buttons. Show them how what you want will satisfy what they want.

This is the recipe for success. Remember Zig's advice — help enough people get what they want so you can get anything you want!

"Don't ask; don't get."

— Gary McDaniel, Entrepreneur,
Son of Rudy McDaniel, Entrepreneur

29

Practice on the Small Stuff

Big wars are won by the winning of many small battles. Big deals are stuck by the stacking of many minor agreements. If you want to learn how to win big in negotiating (and who doesn't?), you must practice every day. This thing called negotiation is an art form gentlemen and ladies; it requires discipline and practice. I'm here to teach you the techniques that will unleash your negotiation creativity. To build the bargaining muscles you'll need to win the big prizes on life's exciting midway — practice your negotiation technique everyday on the small stuff.

Here's a true daily practice story for you. It demonstrates several lessons. First, always be on the lookout for opportunities to practice your bargaining techniques. Next, don't be afraid to be outrageous. And finally, people will give you big discounts if you aren't afraid to ask.

I had a speaking engagement in Keystone, Colorado, in the spring of 2000. After the seminar, I went on a drive with two pals to take in the local sights. We were high atop the Rocky Mountains and had just passed the Continental Divide. Our thirst got our attention and we starting looking for a place to stop for a cold drink. It was still early for tourist season so things were pretty slow but we finally spotted an open ski lodge. There was a cooler full of Pepsi and the like towards the entrance but it was locked. There was a bar towards the very back of the lodge but none of us really wanted to sit down. We just wanted soft drinks to go. So, we got the bartender to come up and unlock the cooler for us.

I was in a good mood hanging out with my buddies and just felt like being silly. "I think I'll have two Diet Pepsi's . . . my treat today guys, what are you drinking?" They fancied a Dr. Pepper and a Coke. The bartender (apparently the owner) dutifully unlocked the cooler and as he was dragging out the liquids the RED ALERT buzzer went off in my head: *small stuff bargaining opportunity at hand, ready the rhetoric.* Almost without thinking, and certainly mostly for a laugh, I blurted out: "How 'bout $3 and we'll be on our way?" My pals blushed and laughed nervously, obviously embarrassed by my foolishness. $3 for four 16-ounce drinks? Don't be ridiculous. Off-season in a resort area, $8 plus tax would have probably been more like it. Good golly, after all, this little joint was the only game in town.

Next I heard the beautiful words: "$3 it is buddy; you must need it more than I do." The mood lightened, everybody laughed; we thanked our new friend and took off in giddy disbelief with our bargain bottles.

Question

If you saved $5 on every $8 purchase from now 'til the day you go to meet your Maker, wouldn't you probably have plenty of extra change in your pocket come Judgment Day?

Now let's review the lessons in this seemingly frivolous exercise.

LESSON ONE

Opportunities abound daily. Practice your bargaining techniques on some of the small stuff every time you get a chance. Your recurring wins will give you confidence for the bigger battles to come.

LESSON TWO

Dare to appear outrageous, even ridiculous. People love it when you make 'em laugh. Humor is often the bridge to agreement. The expression "laughing all the way to the bank" didn't just come out of the void.

LESSON THREE

Don't be afraid to ask. "Don't ask; don't get" as (here he comes again now) my old real estate broker friend, Rudy McDaniel, used to say.

On drinks and wives:
"One's too many and none's not enough."

— Richard R. Rowe, Philosopher

30

Negotiating with Your Significant (Female) Other . . .

Who's got the edge?

All righty then! You read my words. You practiced the exercises I gave you. You had some victories. Your negotiating skills have improved dramatically. Congratulations on your accomplishments!

Now, just when you were beginning to get a manageable handle on higher-level haggling, I'm going to jump way ahead. Here is the ultimate bargaining challenge *any of us* will ever encounter: How to negotiate effectively with your significant other (SO).

Let's assume you are involved in an ongoing relationship with a SO. For simplicity's sake only, let's also assume your relationship is gender traditional (heterosexual).

Whether your relationship is as fresh as spring, in mid-life crisis, or dying on the vine, the simple fact is that you and your SO can't agree on everything. That said, let's bow our heads and jointly acknowledge the reality of the metaphysical and surrealistic nature of relationships.

Friends of both genders, all your hard-earned negotiation skills and equipage, astute understandings and deep insights into human behavior will be of little value to you in this venue. Basically, all bets are off. In this arena it's every woman for herself, every man for himself.

Question

As to gender, who has the home court advantage?

Answer

Sorry, fellows, *you do not*. Studies reveal the fairer sex has the edge! Back in days of Fred and Wilma Flintstone, it appeared that the Freds of the swamp had the dominant gene for winning. (Picture man with club in hand dragging woman by ponytail with other hand).

If you have not already noticed, the days of "might makes right" are over. The battle of the sexes is now being fought on a much more level playing field. Guys, truth be told, there are a whole lot of persons out there of the female persuasion who have studied martial arts and could kick our collective bar brawling and street-fighting butts!

Taking a look back, buds, as little boys we usually prevailed in conflicts by relying on our physical prowess. Brute force was our MO. Our lovelier counterparts, on the other hand, learned how to resolve conflicts with much subtler skills. They obtained the desired results by developing their communication skills. Their "right brain" flourished while ours atrophied. They were solutions-oriented while we were still making threats. They were developing finesse with verbal and non-verbal interpersonal skills while we were still "winning through intimidation".

Now we're all grown up. If you're an average man attempting to resolve an issue of discomfort with your SO here are ten things to remember.

Ten Tips for Negotiating with Your Significant Other

1 Logic just might not serve you well in this instance.

2 Forget what she is saying; listen more to her feelings.

3 Posturing, threatening, yelling, intimidating and hitting are not options.

4 Be gentle; it's your only hope and gentility commands respect.

5 Seriousness, persistence, and the making of demands will fail you.

6 Keep your sense of humor.

7 The best offense is a good defense.

8 Be prepared to deflect her attacks, not with counterattacks, but with kindness.

9 Keep it brief; know when to cut your losses and get out.

10 If she starts to cry, the negotiation is over and guess what? *You lose!!!*

Best of luck, fellows. And, don't forget — you're starting with a distinct disadvantage. So, keep your wits about you and thank the highest power in your life that we're blessed with these lovely beings to keep us on our toes. To quote James Brown, the Godfather of Soul: "This is a man's world . . . but it wouldn't be nuthin', nothing, without a woman or a girl."

> *"We have met the enemy, and the enemy is us."*
>
> — Pogo

31

Getting the VIP Treatment Every Time

You Deserve It!

You *are* a VIP. You deserve the VIP treatment. Preferential service is actually very easy to get. Using the simple tips below will ensure you'll get the royal treatment and red carpet service everywhere you go!

Make an Appointment or Reservation

This makes your arrival an anticipated event. It conveys your high self-esteem. Calling ahead to confirm further enhances your perceived VIP status. It communicates the value you place on your time. Making an appointment or reservation also demonstrates your respect for the service provider's time.

Dress Up

Your clothing and grooming speak volumes about how you expect to be treated. Dressing for success works. A recent *USA Today* "Snapshots" article revealed that only 25% of U.S. travelers dress up and 73% of those felt they got better service when dressed up.

Personalize Yourself

Establishing positive and ongoing relationships is the key for the VIP. Always introduce yourself to front-line employees. Establish rapport by engaging in conversation that displays your knowledge of and interest in their product or service. It is all about winning friends from the bottom to the top.

Become a Regular and Valued Customer

Get to know the owner. Ask about his family. Ask how his business is going. Express your appreciation for his excellent service. Refer your friends.

Be Nice

Please and thank you are still the three magic words of manners. Politeness, gentility and sensitivity work wonders and attract sincere consideration of the highest level.

Address Each Person Who Serves You by Name

Ask the names of the nice folks who help you. Remember each person's name and use it often. Reminder: The most beautiful sound in the world is the sound of another calling us by name. Call the 7-Eleven clerk by name. Look into her eyes. Ask how she's doing. Watch her face light up. Your VIP treatment will evolve each time you do.

Ask Opinions

The people serving you are flattered when you let them know their opinions matter to you. Ask for their expertise. Give them a chance to show off. Make them the star. The paradox is, when you treat them like a star, they treat you like a star. Ask your mechanic's opinion on what brand of oil to use. He'll feel more important in your eyes; you'll be more important in his.

Compliment

Compliments motivate people to go the extra mile for you. Praise your hotel housekeeper for the great job she does. Extra amenities might mysteriously appear in your away-from-home abode throughout your stay.

Be Appreciative

Write a thank-you note. Send a small gift. Demonstrate your appreciation for the VIP treatment that you get. You'll keep getting it.

Be Assertive

You must project the impression that you are accustomed to getting first-class treatment. Remember to complain effectively by prefacing and concluding a complaint with a compliment. Transmit the message that you are not a pushover. "Who's your boss?" is a question that will usually convert bad service into excellent service.

Smile and Use Humor

Smiles send the disarming signal of your approval to another. People honor you in exchange for your approval of them. Their honor confers VIP status upon you. People like doing business with people they like. People like others who make them laugh. A little kidding goes a long way to establish a bond. True and lasting VIP treatment begins with a bond between people.

LESSON

An old saying sums it up. "You can tell a big man by the way he treats a little man." You earn VIP treatment by the way you treat others.

"Never contend with a man who has nothing to lose."

— Baltazar Gracian, *The Art of Worldly Wisdom*

32

How to Negotiate with a Mugger

Show Him the Money

Fact

99% of Americans will be crime victims, or know someone who has been, at least once in their lives. Armed robbery is the most common crime. Reason: Desperate drug addicts mug for money.

These gonzo goons don't typically utilize very sophisticated financial planning techniques, right? Getting cash for the next fix is not usually an issue until after a dope fiend realizes he needs his next fix.

A punk with a "jones" and a "piece" is looking for you right now. Are you prepared?

Three Rules of the Robbers' Road

- You Can't Argue with a Sick Mind. He is not a well-adjusted person. He is also not flexible. Immediately "stipulate" to your willingness to "give it up".

- Never Try to Negotiate with Someone Who Has Nothing to Lose. This has to be one of the most important transactions of your life. Unfortunately, this one is non-negotiable. No amount of money is worth your life. Your adversary (to loosely quote Bob Dylan again) "ain't got nuthin" and "ain't got nuthin' to lose."
- Preparation and Knowledge Will Save Your Life. Prepare mentally and physically now.

You Are Confronted by a Crook with a Gun - What Should You Do?

- Raise your hands in the air. (Police recognize this gesture).
- Say: "I've got money!" (Relax the aggressor).
- Lower your hands, palms out in front of you, admonishing the bandit to STOP. (Keep the hoodlum from progressing into your space).
- Say: "I'm going to get the money for you now." (Notify the gunman you're going to move your hand into your clothing).
- Though time is of the essence, move slowly and smoothly. (Sudden or jerky moves can spook your new friend).
- Pull out the money clip, show the $50, toss it behind the tough on his non-weapon side. (See #10 of "The Ten Knows" on the following page.) The clip prevents wind from blowing "his" money in your direction.
- As the heavy dives for the money, run like #%$.
- Express gratitude. You escaped with your most valuable asset — your life.

The Ten Knows

1. Know it can happen to you.
2. Know sidewalk pirates rely on the element of surprise.
3. Know who looks most vulnerable to crack-crazed criminals: Women carrying purses and men encumbered with packages, etc.
4. Know who looks least vulnerable to dope-demented desperados: Alert folks with erect and confident postures, quick and purposeful gaits.
5. Know when you are the most vulnerable: While unlocking your car door, bent over loading/ unloading your trunk, etc.
6. Know what muggers want: Money (fast).
7. Know what muggers don't want: Jewelry and credit cards. Thankfully, thieves (usually) don't want to hurt you.
8. Know how much your life is worth: More than all the money you carry — that's for sure.
9. Know the going price of illegal drugs: between $20 - $50.
10. Know how to give up the least: Don't carry a purse or wallet. Keep "mug money" (a $50 bill folded in a money clip) where you can access it easily and quickly. (Stash other cash and credit cards elsewhere).

LESSON

Think stipulation not negotiation. Stipulate to your willingness to give up some dough in exchange for escape from a dicey situation. Goal — a smooth, mutually successful transaction. Your preparation, knowledge and composure under pressure will save your life. The best way to end any negotiation is to give your opponent what he wants. In this case, you win! Giving up a few bucks in "mug money" is a small price to pay for your life.

Thanks to Pam Nimitz DeMaris, member of National Speakers Association and author of *Stop the Violence*, for much of the foregoing. Check out her web site at ithesurvivor@flash.net.

33

Chutzpah: Moxie Magic

Refuse to Take NO for an Answer

What is Chutzpah? "Chutzpah is a Yiddish term for gall, brazen, nerve, effrontery, incredible 'guts,' presumption and arrogance," says Idora Silver, author of *The Chutzpah Connection.* (Chutz Press, 800-682-2929).

Famed attorney Alan Dershowitz, author of *Chutzpah*, explains: "To the perpetrator, chutzpah means boldness, assertiveness, a willingness to demand what is due, to defy tradition, to challenge authority, to raise eyebrows."

Moxie Magic

Moxie is another Yiddish term, meaning "bravado". It takes moxie to implement chutzpah.

Chutzpah and Health

Silver shares more: "Chutzpah is healthy for you. It gives you a strong ego, boosts your self-esteem, and helps you toward a life of self-empowerment, decreased stress, increased happiness, and a feeling of individuality and accomplishment."

The Positives of Being "Chutzy"

"Chutzpah can be a positive trait; it is assertive, demanding, and creative." Chutzpah is a good thing. Here are four of Silver's *10+ Traits of Chutzy, Successful People*.

- Creativity: Thinking out of the box requires "growing new eyes". Get different perspectives on the same picture. Play devil's advocate by putting yourself in the other guy's shoes.
- Bravery: Face your fears to overcome negotiating apprehensions. Commit to do what you fear most. Stare down your fears. If you get butterflies — teach them to "fly in formation."
- Persistence: Success is only failure turned inside out. It's not how far you fall but how high you bounce when you hit the ground. You can't hit home runs if you're not willing to strike out once in a while. You gotta walk tall and act successful. Proving your personal prowess takes perennial persistence.
- Risk Taking: Nothing ventured — nothing gained. Don't ask — don't get. Bet on your ability to bargain with the best of them.

The Qualities You Need to Be Chutzy

- ✔ **Boldness:** "Fortune assists the bold" — wise words offered by the poet Virgil. Boldness makes for bodacious, chutzy and dramatic negotiation wins.
- ✔ **Nerve:** This attribute of chutzpah will prevent you from being perceived as weak, timid or enfeebled.
- ✔ **Courage:** True courage is not the brutal force of vulgar heroes — but the firm resolve of virtue and reason. — Whitehead
- ✔ **Gall:** Ask your boss for a raise. Ask for a supervisor when you get bad service. Ask for the moon — you just might get the stars.
- ✔ **Gumption:** Stick to it. Never give up. Dedicate yourself to winning.
- ✔ **Audacity:** Daring delivers self-satisfaction.
- ✔ **Brazenness:** Be shameless in your pursuit of what you want.
- ✔ **Effrontery:** Have the brashness to confront when necessary.
- ✔ **Incredible"Guts":** Gutsy = chutzy.
- ✔ **Presumption:** Possess the pride to project your belief in yourself.
- ✔ **Arrogance:** Develop disdain for the concept of concession.
- ✔ **Assertiveness:** The squeaky wheel gets the grease. Express your needs to get the results you want from others.

Chutzpah Will Give You the Willingness to:

- ✔ **Demand What Is Due:** Don't be a doormat. Convey the value you place on yourself. Require the world to respect your rights.
- ✔ **Defy Tradition:** Refuse to accept "That's our policy", "Those are the rules" and other arbitrary barriers to what you want.
- ✔ **Challenge Authority:** Don't give up your personal power to anyone. Don't let a title intimidate you.
- ✔ **Raise Eyebrows:** Don't be afraid to make a scene. Develop a thick skin. What others think of you is none of your business.

LESSON

Learn to use the moxie magic of chutzpah to get what you want. Don't live with the regrets that "I wish I would have", "I should have" and "If only I'd . . ." bring.

34

Winning with Words

Five to Use and Five to Lose

Psychological researchers tell us how to make our communications more effective. The success of our verbal interactions with opponents in negotiation situations is a function of three variables.

These are not equal in their degree of impact. Here are the variables in effective negotiating and their percentages of relative importance, according to the experts.

- ✔ **15% — What We Say**
- ✔ **35% — How We Say It**
- ✔ **50% — Non-Verbal Behavior**

We're going to look at the "What We Say" variable. There are certain words people just plain don't like to hear. These kinds of words can create deep psychological discomfort. We should all be aware of the images we create with the words we use. It all boils down to positive versus negative. This is especially true in negotiation. We want to provide a negotiating environment with an absolutely positive ambiance. Using the right words creates an attractive atmosphere that magnetizes your opponent to your position.

Here is a list of five words to lose and five more to use in their place.

Words to Lose	Words to Use
Problem	Solution
Decision	Consideration
Try	Results
Maybe	Guarantee
Difficult	Easy

1. **Lose "Problem" — Use "Solution".**

   Problem. People have enough problems. Folks want to feel that dealing with you is going to be trouble-free. Complications, doubts and uncertainties are not desirable.

   Solution. Certainty, surety and solutions elicit more positive responses. Your ability to resolve uneasiness and alleviate pain will undoubtedly be well received.

2. **Lose "Decision" — Use "Consideration".**

   Decision. We all have too many decisions to make. Decisions require responsibility and, goodness knows, none of us need any more responsibility.

   Consideration. Giving something your consideration is a much less threatening proposition than having to make a decision. It implies freedom, flexibility and lack of pressure.

3. **Lose "Try" — Use "Results".**

   Try. Don't you tire of hearing mamsy-pamsy comments like: "I'll try to have it ready for you by four o'clock."? The very transparent "I'll try" is most often synonymous with "I won't".

   Results. Winning words imply a commitment to results. "I'll have it fixed, fixed right and ready to go by four o'clock." is much more reassuring than any "try-talk".

4. **Lose "Maybe" — Use "Guarantee".**

   Maybe. This word implies chance and possibility. It is vague and very non-committal.

   Guarantee. This word implies a promise and security. It is absolute and very reassuring.

5. **Lose "Difficult" — Use "Easy".**

   Difficult. Geez, if something is going to be hard, laborious and strenuous — you would probably want to avoid being a party to such a struggle.

   Easy. Easy is good. Simple is what we want to hear. The whole key in negotiating is: "Make it easy for someone to say 'yes' to you." Using positive words (like easy, solution, consideration, results and guarantee) facilitates your hearing "yes" more and "no" less.

LESSON

The words we choose can make the difference between our winning and losing. To get what you want more often, lose the negative words and use the positive ones. To sum it up about words: "You gotta know when to lose 'em; know when to use 'em."

35

How to Talk Your Way Out of a Traffic Ticket

Ah, come on occifer . . . gimme a break!

The flashing red lights glared in your rearview mirror. You pulled over. Now, the black and white police cruiser is stopped right behind you. The officer is walking up to your car. What should you do? What should you say? Can you talk your way out of a traffic ticket? Here are 14 tips from a former police officer.

✔ **Empathize.** Understand the officer's perspective. Cops assume you are armed and dangerous. "Car stops" are considered life-threatening situations.

✔ **Movements.** Don't make unnecessary movements while you're pulling over. Leaning over to get your paperwork from the glove compartment telegraphs the cop you might be reaching for a weapon.

✔ **Use your turn signal.** This tells the cop you intend to comply with his request to stop.

✔ **Safety.** Pull over to a safe spot where you will not endanger the cop's life.

✔ **Hands.** Keep your hands in plain sight. Do not make sudden moves.

✔ **Stay in your car.** Getting out is considered an act of aggression.

✔ **Paperwork.** Keep your license handy, and the registration and insurance papers clipped together. Be able to find them quickly.

✔ **Comfort.** Your chances of winning increase 50% if the officer feels relaxed. Don't give her any reason to get uptight. Calm officer = negotiable officer.

✔ **Don't argue.** Roadside is not an appropriate venue for argument — court is.

✔ **Courtesy.** Being polite and respectful may earn you a break. It is okay to ask. If the cop isn't receptive, stop your plea short of irritating him.

✔ **Don't lie.** If you get stopped in your own neighborhood, don't tell the cop you didn't know the speed limit.

✔ **Never admit to anything.** Divert the officer's attention to something legitimate that might have distracted you.

✔ **Attitude.** Express disappointment and concern but never anger. Be apologetic. Avoid defensiveness, victim-type allegations of harassment, etc.

✔ **"Pulling rank."** Don't allude to your lofty community stature, your connections with judges or politicians, etc.

Six Officer Questions: "Won't Fly" and "Might Fly" Answers

1. **Officer: What's the hurry?**

   Won't Fly: I'm late for work.

   Might Fly: My wife is having a baby. We're on our way to the hospital.

2. **Officer: Do you know you were going 85 in a 55?**

   Won't Fly: That's impossible man. I had it all the way to the floor and this car doesn't even go that fast.

   Might Fly: Thanks for calling that to my attention officer. I will be more careful.

3. **Officer: Where's the fire?**

   Won't Fly: !&*#. I was really making good time 'til you stopped me.

   Might Fly: No fire, officer. I'm glad you stopped me though. It will be a good reminder.

4. **Officer: Do you know what the speed limit is here?**

   Won't Fly: Yeah, but I was only going a little over.

   Might Fly: I was paying attention but I must have missed the last speed limit sign.

5. **Officer: Do you know how fast you were going?**

   Won't Fly: No. But — no way was I speeding.

   Might Fly: Not exactly but could you tell me so I'll know how close to the limit I was?

6. **Officer: Are you aware you just ran a red light?**

   Won't Fly: I thought red meant "GO".

   Might Fly: I'm sorry officer. I was looking both ways to make sure it was safe to cross the intersection. I guess I just didn't see the light change.

LESSON

This is a psychological game. It is about how the law will be enforced. It is about whether you will benefit from the spirit of the law or whether you will suffer the consequences of the letter of the law.

Remember

You must persuade in the first 10 - 30 seconds.

Bottom Line

The best way to avoid getting a ticket is to obey the law.

36

Negotiating with a Tardy Doctor

Don't Let 'Em Keep You Waitin'

Most doctors are great! Overall, they are unselfish, loyal and dedicated in their quest to keep their patients healthy. On the other hand, there are some less than considerate exceptions. Consider the following.

You have a 2:15 pm appointment with your doctor. You arrange to leave work mid-day and resign yourself to the lost income. You risk your life driving through traffic to ensure getting there on time. You arrive early and check in with the receptionist. You take a seat and flip through an old *Time* magazine.

Shortly, 2:15 comes. You listen attentively for your name to be called — nothing. 2:30, 2:45, 3:00 — you're still not summoned. 3:10 arrives and you're finally called. The MD's underling beckons you back into a small room. He weighs you, then takes your temperature and blood pressure. You answer the obligatory questions about your current medications. Leaving, he relates: "Doctor will be right with you."

3:30, 3:45, 4:00 . . . finally! The door opens and in strides your white-coated medico. One-hour and forty-five minutes late.

No explanation (let alone apology) is forthcoming. You're livid. He asks how you are. You stuff your anger and get down to the business at hand. He listens to your heart with the stethoscope and writes you a prescription. You thank him and, finally, you're outta there.

Guess what? That's not the way it's supposed to be. Your doctor is *NOT* God. In fact, your doc just robbed you. That's right — robbed you. He robbed you of your precious time.

Legally, his office entered into (and obligated him to) a bilateral contract with you. The agreement: He would render services at 2:15 pm and you would pay the bill. You were there on time; he wasn't. Absent a legitimate emergency, his extreme tardiness is totally inexcusable. It is disrespectful and downright rude to keep another human being waiting like that.

Time is your most valuable asset. It is a non-renewable resource.

The Four-Step Cure

The following will empower you to assert your rights and minimize your exposure to this kind of abusive and arrogant treatment.

1. **Demand Respect.** When filling out the initial "Patient History" sheet, scratch out the word "Patient" and replace it with the word "Customer". It *isn't* your job to be "patient". It is the medicine man's job to be on time. Inform the receptionist that you expect (and will settle for nothing less than) timely service.

2. **Call Ahead.** Always call to "confirm" that "Doctor" is running on time before subjecting yourself to having to wait like a dog for a bone.

3. **Confront and Express.** If the practitioner is late, call him

on it. Express your feelings constructively. Provide him the opportunity to justify his breach of contract. Inform him that your time is as valuable to you as his is to him. Assert that you feel insulted and humiliated. Politely ask if he feels an apology might be appropriate. Solicit his commitment that he will take personal responsibility to assure that you will not be the victim of such merciless, unprofessional and, arguably, passive-aggressive behavior in the future.

4. **Reduce the Bill.** Adjust his fee by what the wait actually cost you. Example: Your bill was $87.50. You waited one-hour and forty-five minutes. You make $10 per hour. You actually lost $17.50 (1.75 hours X $10). So, $87.50 (bill) minus $17.50 (lost) = $70.00 (balance to inconsiderate doctor).

Compliment the Punctual Doctor

Again, most doctors are terrific. Always compliment your doctor for being punctual. The concepts expressed above apply only to the very small percentage of the profession that are the exception.

LESSON

Though the foregoing might sound a little extreme, you do deserve respect. Don't give up your dignity, personal power and valued self-esteem by accepting a contract violated by your own doctor. Its okay to remind your health care provider that he is in the people business first and professional practice second. You have my permission.

37

Blowing Away IRS Penalties

You Can Do It Too!!!

Taxes! Ugh!!! Even the best of us get in a tight spot with the taxman now and again. The IRS Code contains 140 penalties. Check out these numbers.

In 1998, IRS assessed over $7 BILLION in penalties.

In 1998, over 34 million individual penalties were assessed.

Your chances of getting assessed a penalty are 1 in 5.

That's the bad news. The good news is that there are lots of ways to beat the penalties. Some sources relate that as many as 50% of assessed penalties are later abated (waived or cancelled).

The two most common penalties are Failure to File (FTF) and Failure to Pay (FTP). FTF is generally 5% per month (25% max). FTP is generally .5% per month (25% max). In the worst of cases, if you owed $1,000 and didn't file and didn't pay until the FTF and FTP maxed — look at the result: FTF (25%) + FTP (25%) = 50%. $1,000 X 50% = $500. No good! And, that doesn't even take into account the IRS interest which *compounds daily.*

Seven Tips To Avoid IRS Penalties

1. Employee — Adjust your Form W-4 if necessary to ensure you'll have enough dollars withheld to cover your tax for the year.
2. Self-Employed — Make adequate quarterly estimated payments so you'll have enough paid in to cover your yearly tax. Credit card payments okay. 888-272-9829.
3. Pay Tax Return Balance Due — Credit card okay. Direct debit option is available if you file electronically. Borrowing from Guido is cheaper than paying IRS penalties.
4. File Even if You Can't Pay — Avoid the 5% FTF penalty.
5. Extensions — File an extension even if you can't pay what you estimate you'll owe. Avoid the 5% FTF penalty. Only requirement: Make a reasonable estimate of what you'll owe. If you can, send partial payment - credit card okay.
6. Form 1127, Extension of Time to Pay Tax — Must pay in full within 30 to 60 days.
7. Form 4571, Explanation for Filing Return Late or Paying Tax Late — Send this form with your late return or late payment. It requests "non-assertion" of penalties. State that you have "Reasonable Cause". Show that there was no willful neglect. (All abatement requests below must show these two things also).

In Notice 746, *Information About Your Notice, Penalty and Interest*, IRS states: "The law lets us remove or reduce the penalties . . . if you have an acceptable reason . . . you may send us a signed statement explaining your reason. We will review it and let you know if we accept your explanation as reasonable cause to remove or reduce your penalty."

Here are ten ways to achieve cancellation of penalties

1. Form 9264
   Request for Abatement of Delinquency or
   Failure to Pay Tax Penalty (Individual)
   Send this form to the IRS Service Center Penalty Abatement Coordinator.

2. Appeal
   If your Form 9264 request (above) is denied, ask to appeal.

3. Tax Court
   If your appeal is denied, ask to go to Tax Court.

4. Interest Abatement
   You can also request interest abatement. You must show that IRS slowed the process by violation of a ministerial or managerial act.

5. Ask a Revenue Officer
   If the IRS collector is in contact with you, ask for penalty abatement.

6. Form 843
   Claim for Refund and Request for Abatement
   You must first pay the tax in full to qualify for this method.

7. District Court or Court of Claims
   If IRS denies your Form 843 claim (above) you can appeal to these two courts. Certain time periods apply.

8. **Taxpayer Advocate Service**
   For taxpayers that have been unable to resolve problems through normal IRS channels. New Hotline: 877-777-4778.

9. **Form 656**
   Offer in Compromise
   New rules even allow the consideration of a compromise in exceptional circumstances such as economic hardship or cases in which not considering a compromise could be considered unfair or inequitable.

10. **Bankruptcy** — Penalties are often discharged or paid pennies on the dollar in bankruptcy.

   To get forms: 1-800-829-3676 or www.irs.gov.

This article has been prepared from sources the author believes to be accurate and reliable. The author is not engaged in rendering legal or accounting advice. The possibility of human or mechanical error does exist. In addition, the facts and circumstances in an individual's particular situation may not be the same as presented here. Laws, regulations, procedures, etc., change frequently. All users of this information are encouraged to do additional research and fact-finding before relying upon the information contained herein.

38

Negotiating With Yourself, The Toughest Sell of All

The Toughest Sell of All

You've probably gotten pretty darn good at bargaining in a lot of situations. Many of us have chalked up some good wins in the heady hinterlands of higher level haggling. Yet, the biggest challenge for each of us with our ever-evolving negotiation expertise is, ironically, negotiating with ourselves. This is the final frontier!

How do you go about winning when it is yourself that you need to persuade? Good question! As a matter of fact, that is the best question you could ask if success and higher personal achievement are your ultimate goals.

Answer: Salesmanship 101 — Overcoming Objections. This is not a difficult job. You just need to acquire and learn to use the right psychological skills. Employing these skills will empower you to overrule the constant stream of unproductive suggestions from your subconscious mind.

Since childhood, you have been negatively programmed.

Result: A huge bank of pessimistic beliefs competes with your valiant attempts to think positively. Prevailing in this tough competition, this negotiation, calls for constant vigilance over your thoughts. *Mental discipline*: You've got to sell yourself on your ability to refute negativity. As the best selling book said: *You Can't Afford the Luxury of a Negative Thought*. So, *PLUS THINK* is the answer!

How to Negotiate for Success by Using PLUS THINK

Positive Self-Talk. You talk to yourself. We all have silent running conversations with ourselves. To win, you've got to monitor this constant self-talk and keep it positive. Remind yourself of your many wonderful qualities, talents and gifts. Converse with yourself about your belief in yourself. Convince yourself that you're a winner. Persuade yourself by recalling your prior successes. Don't berate yourself. Don't let others berate you.

Positive Affirmations. Remember, the subconscious mind always says "yes". Tell it positive things about yourself. It will believe you. "I am great." "I like myself." "I am in control of my life." Just like a computer, this powerful part of your mind executes and colors your actions based upon your input. The results of your actions will be positive if you pre-program properly.

Tell your subconscious mind positive things about life. In return, your perceptions of and responses to life will be positive. As you respond positively to life, life responds positively to you. Success is a vivacious cycle.

Positive Visualization. You gotta believe. If you can see it, you can believe it. If you can believe it, you can achieve it. What the mind can conceive and believe, it can achieve. If you want it, see yourself *with* it.

Goals. The mind is a target-seeking organism. It will influence your every move to facilitate the achievement of your goals. Be clear on your goals. A confused mind always says "no". Set a clear goal and write it down. Review it upon waking and again before retiring each day.

Self-Esteem. Your conception of your value (your self-worth) controls what you experience in life. Building self-esteem is an easy, step-by-step process. Appreciate yourself for all the good things you do. Look at yourself in the mirror and acknowledge your goodness. Forgive yourself for your mistakes. Learn to accept a compliment gracefully. Reward yourself for goals accomplished. Rewards give you incentive to set higher goals and to be more productive. Production is the basis of morale. High morale gives you the strength and confidence to object to negative suggestions and overcome their destructive influences on your positive focus.

LESSON

You can win every time in your negotiations with yourself! Commit to acquire and learn to use the psychological skills above. Make success a vivacious cycle in your life!

"There is less in this than meets the eye."

— Tallulah Bankhead

Afterword

Well, now that you've finished reading the book, here's my question to you. Did you get what you wanted?

Hopefully you've absorbed some handy techniques that are already helping you get more of what you want out of life. My greatest wish is that the skills you got from my stories will make you a bargaining brainchild (even if you felt like a bozo coming in).

I'd really appreciate hearing your comments on what you learned. More importantly, I'd love to hear your success stories. Send me the story of your best bargaining win and you just might see your name in print in the next version of this book.

If I use your story, I'll send you a free copy of the next edition.

Meanwhile, happy trails and . . . always remember: the word "No" is just an interesting opening bargaining position!

—Bobby Covic, EA, Incline Village, Nevada

"The opposite of any correct statement is a false statement. But the opposite of a profound truth may be another profound truth."

— Niels Bohr

Related Resources

YOU CAN NEGOTIATE ANYTHING - The World's Best Negotiator Tells You How to Get What You Want: Herb Cohen. Bantam Books.

WINNING THROUGH INTIMIDATION: Robert J. Ringer. Fawcett Crest.

LOOKING OUT FOR # 1: Robert J. Ringer. Fawcett Crest.

GETTING TO YES: NEGOTIATING AGREEMENT WITHOUT GIVING IN: Robert Fisher and William Ury. Penguin Press.

HOW TO ARGUE AND WIN EVERY TIME: Gerry Spence. St. Martin's Press.

POWER: HOW TO GET IT, HOW TO USE IT: Michael Korda. Ballentine.

I'M OK - YOU'RE OK: Thomas A. Harris, M.D. Avon.

BORN TO WIN: TRANSACTIONAL ANALYSIS WITH GESTALT EXPERIMENTS: Muriel James, Ed.D., and Dorothy Jongewood, Ph.D. Signet.

HOW TO READ A PERSON LIKE A BOOK: Gerald I. Nierenberg and Henry H. Calero. Hawthorn Books, Inc.

THE ART OF NEGOTIATING: Gerald I. Nierenberg. Simon & Schuster, Inc.

NEGOTIATE TO CLOSE: HOW TO MAKE MORE SUCCESSFUL DEALS: Gary Karrass. Simon & Schuster, Inc.

HOW TO GET THE UPPER HAND: SIMPLE TECHNIQUES YOU CAN USE TO WIN THE BATTLES OF EVERYDAY LIFE: Ralph Charell. Stein and Day.

HOW TO OUTNEGOTIATE ANYONE (EVEN A CAR DEALER): Leo Reilly. Adams Media Corporation.

SUCCESS THROUGH A POSITIVE MENTAL ATTITUDE: Napoleon Hill (author of THINK AND GROW RICH) and W. Clement Stone. Pocket.

THE AMAZING RESULTS OF POSITIVE THINKING: Norman Vincent Peale. Crest Book.

PSYCHO-CYBERNETICS: Maxwell Maltz, M.D., F.I.C.S.

THE MAGIC OF THINKING BIG: David J. Schwartz. Cornerstone Library.

THE CHUTZPAH CONNECTION - Blueprint for Success: Idora Silver, CSP. Chutz Press.

HOW TO WIN FRIENDS AND INFLUENCE PEOPLE: Dale Carnegie. Simon & Schuster.

About the Author

Bobby is a U.C. "Bezerkeley" (Berkeley) graduate with a degree in psychology. He worked as a professional musician, rehabilitation counselor for the disabled, real estate broker and casino craps dealer along the way to his current position as a respected author, professional negotiator and prominent tax litigation consultant.

A former columnist for *Deal* magazine, Bobby is also a nationally recognized speaker on matters of negotiation, administrative tax law, practice management, etc. Tens of thousands of professionals attest to the quality of his presentations.

Bobby is a member of the International Association of Professional Negotiators and National Speakers Association. People from all walks of life get a big kick out of his "inside the IRS" stories.

In his "non-tax" persona, Bobby delivers high-content, humorous and fast-paced inspirational presentations — he never fails to motivate his audiences to seek positive changes in their lives.

He always receives excellent evaluations — here are some selected comments from seminar attendees:

"Great advice. Good real-world application of material."
— Robert G. Hartmann, EA

"Thanks for the powerful information and the laughs."
— Tom Buck, CPA

"A life-changing experience . . . enjoyable . . . pertinent . . . both enlightening and entertaining."

— Marcia K. Davis, EA

Bobby also belongs to a host of professional organizations related to his work as an Enrolled Agent (EA*) including the National Association of Enrolled Agents (Nevada and California Societies) and the National Tax Practice Institute Graduate Fellows Association.

* *An EA is an individual who has demonstrated technical competence in the field of taxation and is licensed to represent taxpayers before all administrative levels of the Internal Revenue Service.*

A large portion of his tax litigation consulting practice is devoted to clients with severe IRS difficulties including multi-year failure-to-file and large-dollar collection situations.

Articles referencing Bobby have appeared in the New York Times, Wall Street Journal, San Jose Mercury News, Las Vegas Review Journal, Reno Gazette Journal, and the North Lake Tahoe Bonanza.

NOTES

"Consistency requires you to be as ignorant today as you were a year ago."

— Bernard Berenson

NOTES

"One never goes so far as when one doesn't know where one is going."

— Johann Wolfgang von Goethe

Order Form

Share this collection of true story treasures with others!

PLEASE SUBMIT ORDER VIA

Mail: Pendulum Publishing, POB 6206, Incline Village, NV 89450

Email: bobbycovic@aol.com (credit cards only, please)

Phone: Toll Free, 1-888-687-8197 (credit card only please) or 1-775-831-7694. Fax: 1-775-831-5328.

PLEASE SEND ME:

________ copies of *Everything's Negotiable!* @ $13.95 plus $2.95 each for shipping and handling. Quantity discounts available.

❑ Enclosed is a check or money order (no cash or CODs, please) for $____________ to cover this request.

❑ Please charge this order to my MasterCard or VISA.

Account #: __________________________ Exp.: ___________

Signed: ____

PLEASE SEND THIS ORDER TO:

Name: ____

Mailing Address: _____________________________________

____

Physical Address: ____________________________________

____

Phone: __________________ Email: _______________________

Negotiation Coaching
and
Services

www.Negotiationcoach.net

Bobby Covic offers a negotiation service where he will either coach you, or, if you wish, represent you and negotiate on your behalf.

- IRS, state, county, city or other taxing entity challenges
- Salary and benefits negotiations
- Family disagreements, divorce asset splitting (property settlements), etc.
- Big-ticket items
- Property tax assessment challenges
- Negotiations with creditors, credit clean-up, debt consolidation
- Buying and selling businesses
- Refinancing mortgages, title and escrow fees
- Stock brokerage and real estate agency fees
- Venture capital and private placement terms

Bobby Covic, EA, is also available for keynote speeches, general speaking engagements, corporate purchasing support and negotiation training. He can be reached on bobbycovic@aol.com or 775-831-7694.

Order Form

Share this collection of true story treasures with others!

PLEASE SUBMIT ORDER VIA

Mail: Pendulum Publishing, POB 6206, Incline Village, NV 89450

Email: bobbycovic@aol.com (credit cards only, please)

Phone: Toll Free, 1-888-687-8197 (credit card only please) or 1-775-831-7694. Fax: 1-775-831-5328.

PLEASE SEND ME:

________ copies of *Everything's Negotiable!* @ $13.95 plus $2.95 each for shipping and handling. Quantity discounts available.

❑ Enclosed is a check or money order (no cash or CODs, please) for $____________ to cover this request.

❑ Please charge this order to my MasterCard or VISA.

Account #: ________________________ Exp.: __________

Signed: ____

PLEASE SEND THIS ORDER TO:

Name: ____

Mailing Address: ____________________________________

____

Physical Address: ___________________________________

____

Phone: ________________ Email: ______________________

NOTES

"Nothing will ever be attempted if all possible objections must first be overcome."

— Samuel Johnson